P9-DWW-508

People's Republic of
China

People's Republic of China

BY WIL MARA

Enchantment of the World™
Second Series

Children's Press®

An Imprint of Scholastic Inc.

NEW YORK TORONTO LONDON AUCKLAND SYDNEY
MEXICO CITY NEW DELHI HONG KONG
DANBURY, CONNECTICUT

Frontispiece: Huangshan Mountains

Consultant: Nicole Huang, Director, Center for East Asian Studies, and Associate Professor of
                Chinese Literature
                University of Wisconsin–Madison

Please note: All statistics are as up-to-date as possible at the time of publication.

Book production by The Design Lab

Library of Congress Cataloging-in-Publication Data

Mara, Wil.
  People's Republic of China/by Wil Mara.
      p. cm.—(Enchantment of the world, Second series)
  Includes bibliographical references and index.
  ISBN-13: 978-0-531-25352-6 (lib. bdg.)
  ISBN-10: 0-531-25352-X (lib. bdg.)
  1. China—Juvenile literature. I. Title.
  DS706.M298 2012
  951—dc22   2011011308

People's Republic of
China

Contents

Cover photo:
A Chinese junk

Beijing Opera

Dragon

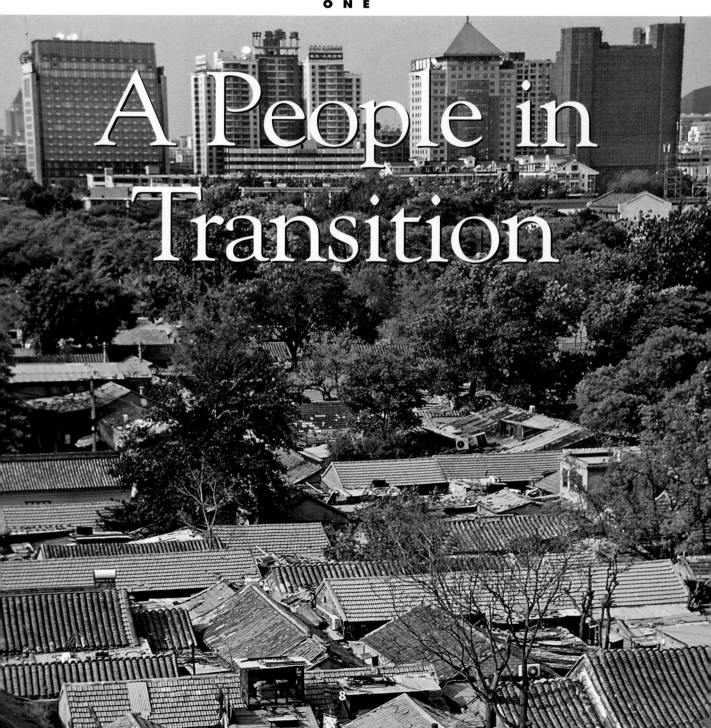

CHAPTER
ONE

A People in Transition

Z HI PENG SNAPS UPRIGHT IN BED AS HIS ALARM CLOCK buzzes on the nightstand. He reaches over and shuts it off with a groan. Looking toward the apartment window, he sees that the sun has barely begun to rise, yet he can hear the street below, already humming with activity. Beijing is not only China's capital but also one of its busiest cities. It is a place of towering skyscrapers, bumper-to-bumper traffic, and nonstop energy. That's why he moved here—that and the fact that there are plenty of legal-profession jobs that pay well. He earned his law degree seven years ago and wanted to make the most of it. There weren't that many fresh young lawyers back then. Nowadays, however, it seems like there are more all the time.

Zhi Peng's wife, Li, is an accountant for a big oil company that is owned and run by the government, and she also makes very good money. She has to get up even earlier than he does, and she's already left for work. They barely get to see each other during the work week, which is usually five days long but, more and more often, stretches into six.

Opposite: **In parts of old Beijing, small houses are clustered together, separated only by narrow alleyways.**

Many Chinese practice tai chi, a form of exercise that involves slow movements.

Zhi Peng walks into the main room of the apartment to do his morning exercises. He has exercised in the morning all his life, but it is difficult here because the room is so small. When he's done, he goes into the bathroom and takes a shower and then gets dressed. As he's tying his shoes, he notices a picture on his dresser. There are many people in it, of varying ages. This is his family back in the Fujian Province, many hundreds of miles south of Beijing.

He grew up on a farm with fourteen relatives, including all four grandparents, two uncles, an aunt, three brothers, and a sister. He has not been back to the farm in almost a year, and

seeing the smiling faces now makes him realize how much he misses them all. His parents were very proud that he got into college. He was the first in his family ever to do so. It took a lot of hard work, and preparing for the entrance exams was so difficult that it stretched his nerves to the breaking point. But he did well and was admitted to one of the best schools in the nation. Now he makes more money than he ever dreamed.

Chinese students study long hours to prepare for the college entrance exams. The tests determine what kind of college they can attend and the career they can have.

He doesn't have time to make an elaborate breakfast. Some bread and yogurt will have to do. He turns on the television as he eats, hoping to catch up on the news of the day. There are many channels, all controlled by the government. He knows the news reports are filtered through their censors; he knows they let the citizens hear only what they want them to hear. This makes him feel a little sad, but there isn't much he can do about it. His parents have told him that the government's control over people's lives used to be much worse.

He checks his watch out of habit, sees that he is late, and darts from the room. He grabs his briefcase and goes out, locking the door behind him. As he steps onto the sidewalk, the bitter scent of polluted air fills his nose. He remembers the fresh country smells that used to greet him every morning back home. So many other memories come to mind—playing in the fields with the animals, swimming in the river at the end of the dirt road, and the smiling faces of the many friends with whom he has since lost touch.

All these thoughts evaporate as the double-decker bus arrives with a groan and squeals to a halt. Melting into the crowd, he works his way to the second floor and finds an empty seat near the back. The bus pulls away and disappears into the morning smog.

People wait to board a bus in Beijing.

Mountains, Deserts, and Plains

CHINA COVERS MORE AREA THAN ALMOST ANY OTHER country in the world. The only two countries that are larger are Russia and Canada. China is larger than the entire continent of Australia and only slightly smaller than Europe. China's total area is about 3,750,000 square miles (9,700,000 square kilometers), but an exact figure is impossible to determine because its political boundaries are in constant dispute.

The View from the Sky

Located in the southeastern part of the Asian continent, China has more than a dozen neighboring countries. Along its northern border, it meets Russia and Mongolia. Along the east, it connects with North Korea. In the south, there is Vietnam, Laos, Myanmar, India, Bhutan, and Nepal. And in the west, a person can cross the Chinese border into Pakistan, Afghanistan, Tajikistan, Kyrgyzstan, and Kazakhstan.

With so many neighboring countries it might be hard to believe China has any shoreline. But it does—along the eastern coast, it touches the Yellow Sea and the East China Sea.

The Jinsha River is the westernmost of three major rivers that flow together to become the Yangtze. The source of the Jinsha River is in southwestern China.

Farther south is the South China Sea. Inland, China has hundreds of other waterways. The best known are the Yangtze River (Chang Jiang in Chinese) and the Yellow River (Huang He). The Yangtze is China's longest river and the third-longest river in the world. It runs crookedly west to east for more than 3,900 miles (6,300 km), through a variety of ecosystems, eventually emptying into the East China Sea. The Yellow River begins in the mountains of western China and finishes at the mouth of the Bohai Gulf, which is part of the Yellow Sea. The Yangtze and Yellow Rivers make the nearby land very fertile.

China's Geographical Features

Area: 3,750,000 square miles (9,700,000 sq km)

Highest Elevation: Mount Everest, 29,035 feet (8,850 m) above sea level

Lowest Elevation: Turpan Depression, 505 feet (154 m) below sea level

Largest Lake: Qinghai Lake, 1,733 square miles (4,489 sq km)

Largest Desert: Gobi, roughly 500,000 square miles (1,300,000 sq km)

Longest River: Yangtze, 3,434 miles (5,527 km)

Highest Average Annual Rainfall: Along the southeastern coast, 80 inches (200 cm)

Lowest Average Annual Rainfall: The northern desert regions, 4 inches (10 cm)

Highest Average Temperature: Turpan, with average July highs of around 116°F (47°C)

Lowest Average Temperature: Harbin, with average January lows of around −1.1°F (−18.4°C)

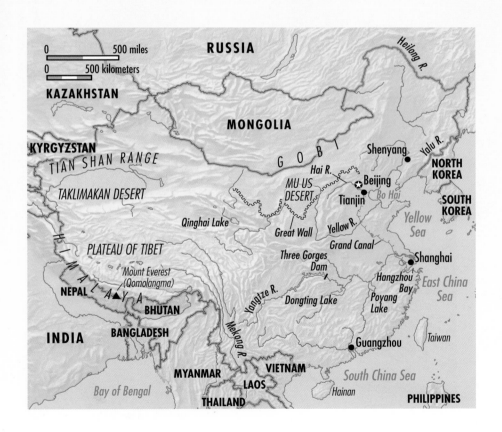

The Tibetan Highlands are found in China's southwestern region. They consist mostly of a vast, hilly plateau surrounded by some of the highest mountain ranges in the world. In fact, the Himalayas, which lie south of the highlands, are home to the highest mountain on Earth: Mount Everest. It rises an amazing 29,035 feet (8,850 m) above sea level. The Tibetan Highlands are also the beginning point for both the Yangtze and Yellow Rivers. The highlands are a rocky, frigid wasteland for much of the year. It is no surprise that they are the least populated area of China.

North of the Tibetan Highlands, in China's northwestern sector, are the Xinjiang-Mongolian Uplands, a stretch of rugged

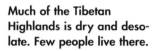

Much of the Tibetan Highlands is dry and desolate. Few people live there.

mountains and bleak deserts. The uplands have many deserts, including the Gobi and the Taklimakan. Sometimes called the Desert of Death, the Taklimakan is one of world's driest deserts.

Running from the northeast into central China are the Mongolian Border Uplands. Much of this region is mountain-ous, harsh, and unpopulated. It also contains the Loess Plateau, which has loose, dry soil. Loess soil is colored by yellowish-brown debris from the surrounding mountains. Some loess ends up in the Yellow River. That's what makes the river yellow.

Starting along China's eastern coastline, and spreading both inland and southward, are the Eastern Lowlands. Miles of flat plains and the valleys of both the Yellow and Yangtze Rivers are found here, providing some of the best farmland in

Part of the Gobi is covered with towering, shifting sand dunes.

The Yellow River flows across northern China for about 2,900 miles (4,700 km). It is the nation's second-longest river.

the nation. Devastating floods used to occur in these areas, but the waterways are now controlled. The Eastern Lowlands host some of China's largest cities, including Shanghai and China's capital, Beijing.

The Eastern Highlands consist of two parts: the Shandong Peninsula, which juts out of China's eastern shore as if reaching for North and South Korea, and eastern Manchuria in China's extreme northeast. The Eastern Highlands are hilly, rocky, thickly forested areas that provide the nation with some of its finest timber, as well as large coal deposits. Mountainous regions in the Manchurian zone form the border between China and North Korea, and the Amur River in the north separates China from Russia.

Bright Lights, Big Cities

Shanghai (below), China's largest city with a population of about 18 million people, lies on the eastern coast at the mouth of the Yangtze River. Shanghai became a major trading port in the nineteenth century, and many Europeans worked there. Today, parts of the city still have a European flavor, and it remains important for shipping and trade. Some of the world's tallest skyscrapers soar into the sky in the Pudong part of the city. At 1,614 feet (492 m), the Shanghai World Financial Center is the third-tallest building in the world.

Beijing, the capital, is China's second-largest city, with a population of about 13.2 million. The nation's third-largest city, Guangzhou (above), is home to about 12 million people. It lies in southern China along the Pearl River. The city, once called Panyu, was founded in 214 BCE. Guangzhou grew and prospered, and by the 1700s it was a great trading port. Until 1842, it was the only Chinese port open to foreign trade, and it remains an important port today. It is also a center of manufacturing.

Farmers have cut terraces into some hillsides to create more flat land on which to plant crops.

The Central Uplands lies between the Tibetan Plateau and the Eastern Lowlands. The Qinling mountain range is the most prominent feature in this region. The range runs east-west and divides the dry land in the north from the warm, humid areas of the south. It also blocks cold northern winds from penetrating the semitropical south, and the southern moisture from interfering with weather patterns in the north.

Just south of the Central Uplands is the Sichuan Basin. It is a place of countless hills and valleys, all surrounded by more mountain ranges. Due to its geographic isolation, warm climate, and many rivers, it is one of China's richest agricultural regions. The Yangtze River flows through the southern part of the basin. The Sichuan Basin is also home to Chongqing, one of China's busiest cities. It lies along the Yangtze and is home to more than 7.5 million people.

A Giant Flood Zone

Many strong rivers snake through China. As a consequence, flooding is all too common. In fact, many of the worst floods in world history occurred in China. The deadliest flooding of all time happened in 1931. Snowmelt from a harsh winter followed by continual rains and an unusually large number of major storms caused the Yellow, Yangtze, Huai, and other rivers to spill over. At least 1.5 million people died. Some estimate the number of dead at twice that. No matter which number is more accurate, the 1931 floods were the deadliest natural disaster in human history. Similar horrors took place in 1887, when the Yellow River overflowed and claimed roughly 1.5 million lives. In 1938, the Yellow swelled again, killing about half a million people.

China's Southern Uplands occupies just about all of the nation's southwestern sector. This is a land of warm, semitropical and tropical environments, and a seemingly unending string of hills. The most level area is found around the Pearl River delta in the nation's southeastern corner, where the Pearl River flows into the South China Sea. Many of China's most populated cities are located near the Pearl River delta, including Guangzhou, Shenzhen, Macau, and Hong Kong. The rural parts of the delta and other stretches of the Southern Uplands have provided ideal farming conditions for centuries.

China's Islands

China controls vast numbers of islands that lie off its eastern and southeastern shores. The Zhoushan Archipelago (right) alone has more than 1,300 tiny islands, and Hong Kong has more than 200 others. Hainan Island is one of the nation's largest and most important. It is located off the southern coast and is home to eight large cities, including Haikou.

From Hot to Cold

In China, the climate varies tremendously depending on the region. It is helpful to think of China in three sections—northern, middle, and southern. In warm seasons, all three sections have similar climates. But during the winter, there are often big differences.

Many of China's towering peaks are covered with snow year-round.

Cars park on the beach at Dalian in northeastern China. People flock to China's beaches during the summer.

Northern China can be fairly comfortable in both the warm and cold seasons, with temperature swings similar to those found in the northern United States and southern Canada. The upper north of China, however, is a different story. The deserts there can be brutally hot during the height of summer, with daytime temperatures reaching above 100 degrees Fahrenheit (38 degrees Celsius). These same areas can drop to below zero during the winter.

A man rides a motorcycle through flooded streets in southern China following a storm.

Throughout much of central and southwestern China, where the climate is subtropical, temperatures usually range from around 80°F (27°C) in the warmer months to 39°F (4°C) in winter. In areas surrounded by mountain ranges, summers are usually cooler and winters gentler.

Southeastern China features hot and humid conditions in the spring and summer, with an average temperature of about 80°F (27°C).

One of the greatest factors affecting China's climate are monsoon winds. These powerful gusts blow from different directions depending on the time of year. In the fall and winter, they drive down from the frigid north, causing severe drops in temperature and humidity throughout much of China's north and north-central regions. In the spring and summer, they roll off the Indian Ocean hundreds of miles to the south, move across India, and reach into southern China, carrying warm rains that may fall for weeks in some areas. Seasonal warm winds from the Pacific Ocean also cross China's eastern and southern borders and move inland, bringing even more rain and humidity. Monsoons are responsible for rainy seasons, and in some cases drive destructive tropical cyclones called typhoons. In the Atlantic Ocean, similar storms are known as hurricanes.

Dirty Water

Can you imagine being unable to find clean water? Many people in China face this nightmare every day. The nation's huge population and pollution from rapid industrial development are the main causes of this problem. In 2008, the environmental organization Greenpeace tested water supplies around China and found 80 percent to be undrinkable. Hundreds of cities are currently dealing with shortages, and millions of people in rural areas drink unsafe water every day.

Living Things

B
ECAUSE CHINA HAS A HUGE VARIETY OF ENVIRONMENTS, it also has an amazing variety of plant and animal life. Thousands upon thousands of species live in the country, and many more have yet to be discovered. Scientists have not even explored some of the remote areas of the country.

Opposite: **Conifer trees grow high in the Huangshan Mountains of eastern China.**

From the Ground Up

China is home to more than thirty thousand plant species—more than 10 percent of the world's total. This number was even greater in centuries past, but growing cities and industries have taken a heavy toll. In the twentieth century alone, industrialization and expanding farms have caused many species to become extinct. Nevertheless, China remains a biological treasure trove where plant life is concerned.

The chilly mountain regions of the north are covered with conifer (cone-bearing) trees in many areas. In the extreme northeast, the heart of China's timber industry, larch trees are plentiful. Other northern regions have tough, weedy grasses

The Beloved Peony

China does not have an official national flower, but one is closely associated with China: the peony. Many peonies are fragrant. They are fairly easy to raise, and they blossom in striking shades of red, gold, or white. There are dozens of species of peonies. Some grow on bushes, others on trees. The finest peonies are grown in the ancient city of Luoyang. In 1994, the peony won a national poll as the favorite floral symbol of the nation.

that survive on little warmth or moisture. Much of the plateau areas are equally sparse, particularly at higher elevations.

More temperate regions, which are similar to those in the United States and Canada, feature trees such as elm, oak, and

Lucky Bamboo

Bamboo is one of the plants most commonly associated with China. Although it is tall and rigid, it is not, in fact, a tree. Instead, it's a type of grass. Bamboo is found in the warmer, southern parts of the country, usually in dense clusters. It is among the fastest-growing of all plant species. Some varieties can grow more than 3 feet (1 m) in a single day. Bamboo lives twenty to more than one hundred years, and some stretches of bamboo forest have been standing for centuries. Thus, many people in China consider bamboo a symbol of luck and long life. Bamboo is also important to the Chinese economy. It is used in medicine, food, clothes, landscaping, and construction.

maple. Bamboo and ginkgo trees thrive in China's subtropical areas. Tropical regions feature rain forests. The plant life here is lush and vibrant, often with thick, broad leaves. Some trees grow more than 120 feet (35 m) tall.

One tree that thrives in tropical and subtropical areas is the mandarin orange. The tree grows only about 10 to 15 feet (3 to 4.5 m) high. It has a narrow, spindly trunk that gives it a somewhat fragile appearance, yet it is actually remarkably

The Chinese have been growing mandarin oranges for thousands of years.

hardy during stretches of dry weather. The fruit, however, is more delicate and must be picked during its short period of ripening. China is the world's leading producer of mandarin oranges. The Chinese use the oranges in a variety of ways. They eat them as snacks. They give them as gifts during Chinese New Year because they symbolize good fortune. The peel is also believed to have medicinal value.

All Kinds of Creatures

China boasts a startling array of animal life that includes more than 500 different mammal species, 1,200 bird species, and 3,800 fish species. China has a little of everything: hoofed mammals such as antelope, deer, and horses; meat eaters such as tigers, bears, and alligators; elegant and colorful birds such as parrots, peacocks, pheasants, and cranes; and many creatures of the sea, including salmon, tuna, clams, and oysters.

Ancient Trees

The dawn redwood tree grows only in two provinces in south-central China. Related to the towering giant sequoia of the United States, it grows to an average height of about 200 feet (60 m). The dawn redwood was thought to be extinct until a small number were discovered in the mid-1940s. Since then, scientists have gathered its seeds and grown new trees. The dawn redwoods that still exist in the wild are protected by law. Scientists have found fossils of the dawn redwood tree throughout the Northern Hemisphere. This suggests that the few trees remaining in China are all that is left of a once widespread population.

The Beijing Zoo is one of the oldest, largest, and most impressive zoos in China. Founded in 1906, today it houses nearly fifteen thousand animals in exhibits ranging from mountains and meadows to indoor rain forests and giant aquariums. It is also home to some of the most beautiful flower gardens in the nation. Among its many animal residents are a few of the rarest species in China, such as the giant panda, the Père David's deer, the Chinese alligator, and the golden snub-nosed monkey (left). The zoo also features rare species from other parts of the globe, including kangaroos, chimpanzees, elephants, and sea turtles. Besides being a place for people to get a close-up view of animals, the zoo is also a scientific research center and hosts a number of breeding programs critical to the survival of the nation's most endangered species.

The yak lives in China's chilly northern regions. It is a shy, shaggy, cowlike creature related to the bison of North America. In the steamy southern rain forests lives the gibbon, a member of the ape group. The gibbon shows remarkable speed and agility when swinging between vines and branches. The gibbon has long been hunted, and many of the forests where it once lived have been cut down. Because of this, the gibbon has become rare in many parts of China.

Equally rare is the giant panda. A member of the bear family, it has won over the hearts of millions because its round face and body and distinctive black-and-white markings make it look like a stuffed animal. The average adult giant

Creeping Giant

Most salamander species are small, measuring only a few inches long. China, however, is home to a monster salamander. The Chinese giant salamander grows to more than 3 feet (1 m) long and weighs more than 60 pounds (25 kg). It lives in mountain lakes and streams, where it feeds on whatever crawls or wiggles by, including fish, frogs, and insects. The salamander has a grayish, mottled appearance and a round head that looks like a rock. Its appearance helps it hide from other creatures. This gentle, slow-moving animal is in grave danger of extinction. It has been collected by the thousands, sold as a pet, and eaten as food. Habitat loss and pollution have also harmed the salamander.

panda grows to about 5 feet (1.5 m) in length and weighs about 300 pounds (135 kilograms). The giant panda lives in bamboo forests in the mountain ranges of central China. Bamboo, in fact, makes up the great bulk of its diet, although it occasionally eats other plants or animals. The giant panda

Giant pandas eat for up to fourteen hours a day.

spends most of its time on the ground, but it scurries up a tree if alarmed. Despite their toylike appearance, pandas can be ill-tempered toward people. Expanding human settlements have greatly reduced the population of giant pandas, and now perhaps only a few thousand remain in the wild.

Another beautiful but rare Chinese mammal is the snow leopard. Living high in rocky mountain regions, it is well suited to cold weather. It has thick fur, wide paws that allow it to walk on top of snow, and small ears so it doesn't lose too much body heat through them. The snow leopard cannot roar. Instead, it mews, hisses, and growls. The snow leopard is most active at sunrise and sunset, and even then it remains extremely secretive. Because of this, scientists have had a hard time determining exactly how many remain in the wild. China is believed to have only a few thousand snow leopards.

Employees at Wolong National Nature Reserve in south-central China show off giant panda babies. The reserve is home to about 150 giant pandas.

Making a Difference

In the early 1980s, a group called the China Wildlife Conservation Association (CWCA) was founded. Its mission is to preserve China's wildlife, mostly through public education, scientific research, breeding programs, and protecting the environment. Members of the CWCA visit schools and community centers to raise awareness about the dangers facing China's wildlife. One of their main goals is to convince people not to eat wild animals, particularly those that are in danger of extinction. Today, the CWCA has more than six hundred regional branches and two hundred thousand members.

Through the Centuries

I F YOU WERE TO COMPARE THE HISTORY OF CHINA WITH that of the United States, China would be like a great-grandfather and the United States would be a toddler. When the United States declared its independence in 1776, China had already been around for many thousands of years. Some structures still in use in China are thousands of years older than the United States. China is, in fact, one of the oldest civilizations in the world. It has gone through periods of great upheaval and instability, of suffering and sorrow. But it has also seen times of remarkable cultural beauty, intellectual achievement, and technological innovation.

Opposite: **Beijing's Temple of Heaven was built in the early 1400s as a site for the emperor to hold ceremonies praying for a good harvest.**

From the Beginning

Scientists believe that early hominids—forerunners of today's human beings—lived in what is now China over a million years ago. At that time, hominids were already making use of stone tools and fire. Humans similar to modern people appeared in China around two hundred thousand years ago.

This cart and the horse bones were discovered in Henan Province in central China. They are more than two thousand years old.

Eventually, people learned to grow and store crops such as rice and millet and to domesticate animals such as pigs and cattle. They also began establishing villages, many along the Yellow River. By 6000 BCE, people in China were making art. By 3500 BCE, the Chinese were making silk.

The Magic of Silk

The Chinese were the first people to produce the shimmering fabric called silk, and they long guarded the secret of how to make it. To make silk, you need both silkworms (a kind of caterpillar) and mulberry trees (silkworms only eat mulberry leaves). Silkworms eat nonstop and grow quickly. After they have grown, they spin a cocoon. Each cocoon is made from a single strand of silk, some of which are 3,000 feet (900 m) long. To harvest the silk, the cocoons must be soaked in boiling water and then unwound. Strands of silk are combined to make a thread, and the thread is woven into cloth.

Early Dynasties

For centuries, China was ruled by dynasties. A dynasty is a line of leaders, usually from the same family. Some dynasties lasted hundreds of years, others just a few decades. The transition between dynasties was sometimes violent. One dynasty often had power ripped from its grasp. Revolution and instability were common. The nation sometimes became fragmented into smaller political sections, only to be reunited by the next dynasty. For better or worse, each of these dynastic periods had its own unique characteristics, and each contributed to the China of today.

This small bronze bell is about four thousand years old. It dates to China's first dynasty, the Xia.

The Shang emperor was a military leader. In this print, the emperor battles his enemies.

The first ruling family was the Xia dynasty, which lasted some five hundred years, from around 2000 to 1500 BCE. During this period, some of China's earliest towns were built. During the Xia dynasty, Chinese people began using boats, carts, and weapons, such as bows and arrows. They domesticated horses, began digging irrigation channels, kept track of days on a calendar, and began using written symbols to communicate.

Following the Xia was the Shang dynasty. It also lasted roughly five hundred years, from around 1500 to 1000 BCE. The Shang were considered both military and religious leaders. Many people believed they had the power to see into the future by reading the cracks in animal bones. During the Shang dynasty, a formal government also began to take shape.

The Zhou dynasty followed the Shang and continued until 221 BCE. It was during this time that laws were first written down, farmers began using oxen to pull their plows, and coins were created to use as money. This was also an age of great thinkers, such as Laozi and Confucius, who debated philosophies and searched for a new and better way of life. The Zhou dynasty saw the dawn of the feudal system. Under this system, kings gave control of certain regions (states) to people who were loyal to them. In 770 BCE, some states rebelled, and the Zhou leaders were forced to flee. Zhou kings still ruled after that, but without as much power and influence.

The Zhou dynasty was followed by one of the shortest dynasties, the Qin. It lasted just fifteen years, from 221 to 206 BCE. It was ruled by the brutal Qin Shihuangdi, who brought the fractured states from the Zhou back together through ruthlessness. He declared himself an emperor rather than a king, becoming the first of a long line of Chinese leaders to use that title. Qin

Wise Guy

Confucius, a great philosopher and teacher, was born in the sixth century BCE. Though he grew up in poverty, he become a government minister. After seeing political corruption firsthand, he left his post and began traveling around China, encouraging people to behave in an ethical and moral fashion. By the time of his death in his early seventies, he had gained a small following that would grow in the years ahead. To this day, many short proverbs are attributed to Confucius, such as "A great soul is never friendless, for he always has neighbors." Whether or not he actually wrote these inspiring sayings is unknown, for none of his actual writings still exist.

Qin Shihuangdi had a tomb built for himself that featured thousands of clay soldiers, hundreds of horses, and more than a hundred chariots. All are life-size.

Shihuangdi killed off many elites so that no one would threaten his power. He outlawed some books and had hundreds of scholars murdered. He also expanded China's size by acquiring many new territories, many through sheer force. Qin Shihuangdi also worked to improve China. Under his leadership, the Chinese language and units of measure were standardized, new roads and waterways were built, and work began on the Great Wall of China. He also had a tomb built for himself that featured a vast army of clay figures. After Qin Shihuangdi died in 210 BCE, his son took over. But the son did not inspire the same fear as his father, and he soon lost political control.

The Lost Army

In the spring of 1974, while digging a well in the Shaanxi Province in central China, a group of farmers made one of the most astonishing archaeological discoveries in history—a statue "army" of more than eight thousand soldiers and five hundred horses made of terra-cotta (a baked and unglazed clay). Further digging revealed that the terra-cotta army was part of the burial site of China's first emperor, Qin Shihuangdi. It is believed he ordered the construction of the army to help him rule another land after his death. The terra-cotta army is extraordinary. No two soldiers are alike, and each bears remarkable details.

The Han dynasty began in 206 BCE and lasted for more than four hundred years, until 220 CE. During the Han dynasty, the philosophy of Confucius grew in importance. Many people who were well-versed in Confucianism received important government positions so they could help shape the nation's policies. The religious teachings of Buddhism also began to take hold during this time. China began trading with the neighboring peoples of central Asia. As people trekked back and forth across Asia, they established a network of routes known as the Silk Road.

A period of instability followed the Han dynasty. China became divided into three areas—Wei, Shu, and Wu—so this period is sometimes called the Three Kingdoms. Confucianism began to fade during this time. Buddhism and another school of thought, called Daoism, were on the rise.

In this painting on silk, the emperor's boats sail on the Grand Canal during the Sui dynasty.

The Sui dynasty followed the Three Kingdoms period. It lasted just thirty-seven years, from 581 to 618. It began with Yang Jian, a government official and Buddhist who reunified China and took the title Emperor Wen. He launched the construction of the Grand Canal, which linked the Yangtze River to the Huai River, and provided a useful channel for shipping and trade. He also ordered that examinations based on a knowledge of Confucianism be required for government posts. This meant that anyone, not just friends and relatives of existing government officials, had a chance to get a job in the government.

Celebrated Time

The Tang dynasty, which lasted from 618 to 907, was one of the most celebrated in China's history. It was a period of inspired thinking, cultural exchange, and political expansion, elevating China into one of the great centers of the world. Visitors of all sorts—students, traders, missionaries—came to China. This exposed the Chinese people not only to the habits and customs of foreign lands but also to new ideas and innovations. Chinese art flourished. Some of China's greatest poets lived in this age, including Li Po, Wang Wei, and Du Fu.

Buddhism's influence diminished during this time, making room for religious beliefs imported from abroad. Some of these new religions included Christianity, Judaism, and Islam. But toward the end of the Tang period, Buddhism regained popularity. It grew so much that the government tried to repress it by destroying thousands of Buddhist temples and monasteries. This caused many Chinese to lose faith in the Tang leadership, which contributed to the end of the dynasty.

During the Tang dynasty, massive Buddhist carvings were made at Dazu Rock near Chongqing. The site includes more than fifty thousand carvings.

These coins date back to the Song dynasty.

Later Dynasties

From 907 to 960, five different military regimes tried to seize power in China. This led to another fracturing of the nation into several parts. (This era is sometimes called Five Dynasties and Ten Kingdoms.) There followed a period of widespread corruption and hardship for ordinary citizens.

The Song dynasty began in 960 and lasted until 1279. It was similar to the Tang in that it ushered in another period of growth and development. A central government was formed, and many new cities arose as centers of trade and industry. The population grew to more than 100 million during this time. Unfortunately, most Song leaders were highly educated but unrealistic. They were often ill-prepared to deal with the difficulties of such a large nation. The people who ruled the country ran out of money. With a weakened military due to the lack of funds,

China became ripe for invasion. In 1215, an army of Mongols from China's north, led by Genghis Khan, captured the city of Beijing. The Mongols gradually conquered the rest of the nation.

The Yuan dynasty began in 1279 under the leadership of Kublai Khan, grandson of Genghis, and lasted until 1368. It was the first time that China was ruled by someone not of Chinese origin. Under Kublai Khan's rule, government posts were given to

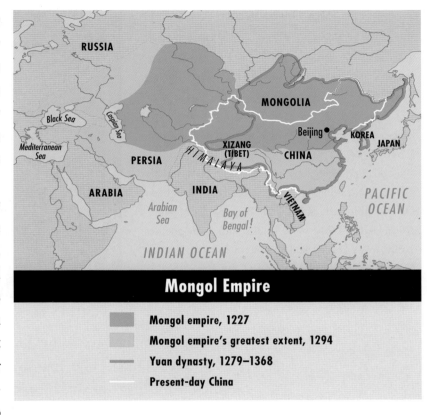

Mongol Empire

- Mongol empire, 1227
- Mongol empire's greatest extent, 1294
- Yuan dynasty, 1279–1368
- Present-day China

many non-Chinese, including Russians and Persians. Foreigners flooded into the nation, and Kublai Khan welcomed them, confident that China was now firmly part of the Mongolian Empire. Eventually, there was an uprising, and growing internal squabbles by Kublai Khan's military leaders led to the end of his reign.

The Ming dynasty followed from 1368 to 1644. With it came a return to Chinese traditions lost during the Yuan. The Mongols were forced out, and the arts were once again practiced and celebrated. To reduce the threat of future interference from the Mongols, the Great Wall of China was expanded. There

The Great Wall

The Great Wall of China is the nation's most famous landmark. Construction began in the second century BCE. The wall's purpose was to defend against attacks from groups to the north. The Great Wall was extended in the centuries that followed. The largest portion was built during the Ming dynasty (1368–1644) to repel raids by Mongol invaders. Wall-building technology had advanced considerably by this time, and the Ming sections have always been the strongest parts of the wall. The wall's final length is just under 3,900 miles (6,300 km), with another 1,600 miles (2,600 km) of natural barriers such as trenches, rivers, and hills. Today, the Great Wall is one of China's most popular tourist attractions.

was also tremendous economic growth and prosperity, and the population doubled. The nation's capital was established at Beijing for the first time in the early fifteenth century. Another first occurred during the Ming dynasty: interaction between Chinese and Europeans.

The final Chinese dynasty was the Qing, which began when Beijing was captured by the Manchus. It lasted for nearly three centuries, from 1644 until 1912. The Manchus made an effort to retain Chinese customs. The nation expanded farther, and the economy and trade grew. The population continued to skyrocket, reaching 300 million by the end of the eighteenth century, and more than 400 million by the middle of the nineteenth century. With so many people, problems grew. There was not enough money, not enough food, not enough land.

People suffered and grew bitter. Then foreign powers from around the world took control of certain parts of China. Hong Kong, for example, fell under the rule of Great Britain in 1842. It wasn't long before France, Russia, Japan, and the United States got involved. By 1911, dissatisfaction had reached a boiling point among the people. Revolutionary groups began working to change the form of government. The last Qing leader lost power, and the age of dynasties in Chinese history came to an end.

The Modern Era

The Republic of China was established in 1912 following the revolutionary uprising of the previous year. A series of battles for leadership followed. New political parties emerged.

Nationalist leader Chiang Kai-shek inspects his troops.

Mao Zedong (left) was the most influential person in China in the twentieth century. He led the Communist Party of China for more than thirty years.

Chiang Kai-shek, one of the founders of China's Nationalist Party—known as the Guomindang—took command of the party in 1925. He wanted absolute rule over the nation.

But many people opposed him. Some belonged to the Communist Party of China (CPC). They believed that the government should own businesses and control the economy. The Communists eventually united under a man named Mao Zedong. The Communists were fewer in number than the Nationalists, and they had less money and equipment to win a war, but they were committed.

Chiang Kai-shek attempted to eliminate the threat the Communist Party posed to his power. His supporters drove out as many Communists as they could. In 1934, the Communist troops made a retreat to evade Chiang Kai-shek's forces. In what is known as the Long March, the Communists in southern China escaped to the north and the west across some of China's harshest and most unforgiving land. Over the course of a year, they walked 6,000 miles (10,000 km). During the march, the Communists met many poor peasants. The peasants were impressed by their bravery and determination, and many joined their cause.

Only twenty thousand of the one hundred thousand Communist troops who started the Long March completed it. One of those was Mao

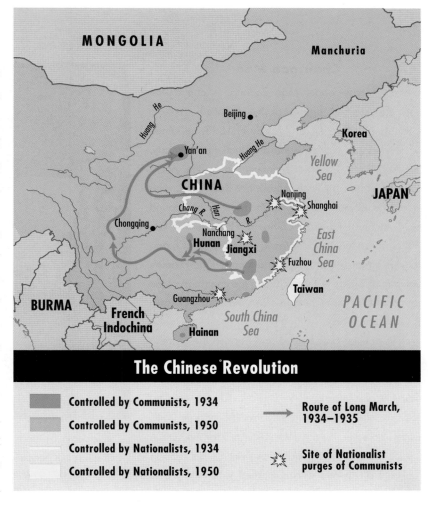

The Chinese Revolution

- Controlled by Communists, 1934
- Controlled by Communists, 1950
- Controlled by Nationalists, 1934
- Controlled by Nationalists, 1950
- → Route of Long March, 1934–1935
- Site of Nationalist purges of Communists

Zedong. The march cemented his reputation as a master military strategist and strong leader. It also proved that peasants would fight for Communism.

In the 1930s, Japan had been trying to expand into Chinese territory. China and Japan went to war in 1937. This eventually became part of the larger conflict known as World War II (1939–1945). During the war, the Communists and Nationalists both worked to stop invading Japanese forces.

Chairman Mao

Former Chinese leader Mao Zedong, is one of the most controversial figures of the twentieth century. Born into a well-to-do rural family in 1893, he joined the revolutionary forces against China's final dynasty, the Qing, in 1911. Heavily influenced by the teachings of German political philosopher Karl Marx, who wrote *The Communist Manifesto*, Mao helped found the Communist Party of China in 1921. In the late 1940s, following World War II, he drove out Chiang Kai-shek's Nationalist troops and founded the People's Republic of China. After becoming the chairman of the Communist Party of China in 1954, he became known as Chairman Mao.

His policies both helped and harmed the Chinese people. He led the transition from a mostly agricultural economy to one with powerful manufacturing industries. He also attempted to improve China's eroding infrastructure by building new roads, bridges, and canals. However, his complete disregard for the human cost of many of his policies, as well as his ruthless treatment of anyone who disagreed with him, led to

the death of more than forty million Chinese. Despite this, many people in China still consider him a hero. He died in 1976.

Communist Victory

After World War II ended, Communists and Nationalists battled for control of the nation. The civil war continued until 1949, when the Communists took control of Nanjing, the Nationalist capital. Chiang Kai-shek and the Nationalists fled. On October 1, 1949, Mao Zedong proclaimed the founding of the People's Republic of China.

Two Chinas

Following their defeat by Mao Zedong's forces in China's civil war, Chiang Kai-shek and his followers fled to the nearby island of Taiwan, where they maintained the government of the Republic of China. Many of those who fled to Taiwan had been leaders of China's business and intellectual communities. Taiwan eventually became a major economic force in the region. Unlike mainland China, which had a Communist economic system, Taiwan was capitalist. Private individuals owned the businesses. Chiang Kai-shek died in 1975, but the Republic of China continues. Some leaders of Taiwan insist that they are, in fact, China's true government. Taiwan still flies the old Republic of China flag, which was first used in 1928.

The new Communist government soon took over important industries. Land was taken away from farmers. Before long, not enough food was being produced to feed all the people. By the late 1950s, China was suffering from severe food shortages, or famine. To stop anyone who threatened his power, Mao began a movement called the Cultural Revolution. The purpose of the Cultural Revolution was to remove any power that the elite had in Chinese society. Scientists, artists, teachers, and politicians were all considered elite. They were sent to the country for "reeducation." This meant hard labor. Anyone who had not always been a complete Mao supporter was in danger. Finally, after ten years of turmoil, the Cultural Revolution ended. Life eventually returned to normal.

A portrait of Mao Zedong hangs in Tiananmen Square in Beijing.

Mao Zedong died in 1976. Deng Xiaoping became the new leader of China. During his twenty-one years in power, Deng began allowing more economic and religious freedom. Slowly, the country was changing.

Democracy was still a distant dream, however. In 1989, students began gathering in Tiananmen Square, a large plaza in Beijing. They were protesting government corruption and calling for greater democracy. After several weeks of protests, the

Chinese army fired on the protesters. Hundreds, and possibly thousands, of demonstrators were killed. Governments around the world criticized China for its violence.

In the years since, China has improved relations with other countries. More private enterprise and more foreign investment is being allowed by the leadership, and China is now integrated into the world economy.

In 2008, the eyes of the world turned toward China, when Beijing hosted the Summer Olympics. The Games were considered a great success. Although China is still frequently criticized for not allowing its people political freedom and the right to criticize the government, it is now firmly established as one of the world's great superpowers.

Beijing National Stadium was built for the 2008 Olympics. It is nicknamed the Bird's Nest.

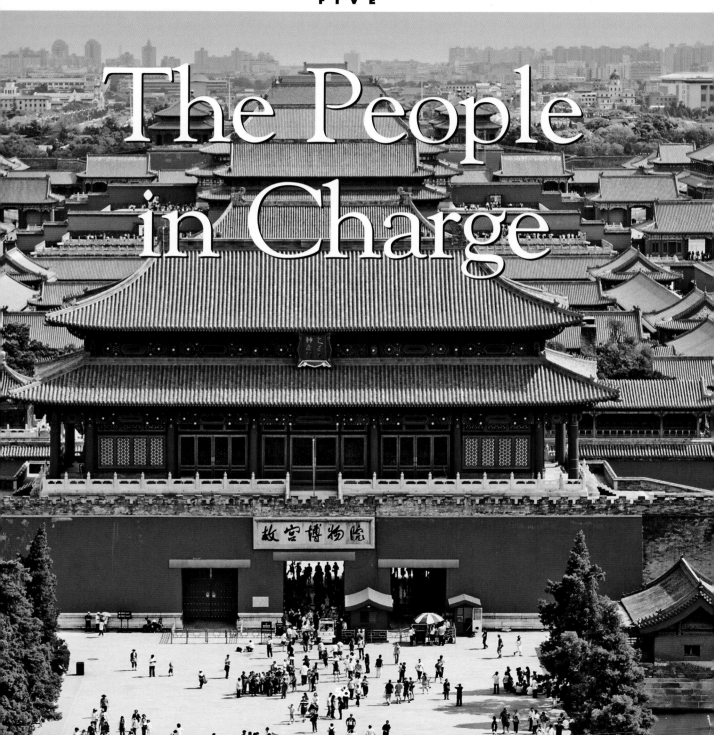

The People
in Charge

O N THE SURFACE, THE GOVERNMENT OF CHINA MIGHT seem similar to that of the United States. It collects taxes, provides an array of services, and maintains an army. Like the U.S. government, it has three branches—executive, legislative, and judicial. Looking closer, however, some startling differences emerge. For example, although China claims to have several political parties, in reality, only one calls the shots. The United States has two major parties, with various third parties that sometimes affect the government. Also, the people of China have relatively little say in who holds political office. The Chinese system is mostly based on appointments rather than on public elections, like those held in the United States or Canada. These factors mean that Chinese people have little say in their government. In recent years, however, the Chinese government has taken tiny steps toward a more democratic society.

Opposite: **When China had dynasties, the Forbidden City in the middle of Beijing was the emperor's residence. It is the world's largest palace.**

The Pieces of the Puzzle

For the purposes of practical governing, the nation of China is broken down into smaller sections. At the highest level is a

Macau was once a Portuguese colony, and parts of the city still have a strong European feel.

division called a province, which is similar to a Canadian province or a U.S. state. China has twenty-two provinces. It also includes five autonomous—largely self-governing—regions on the provincial level. They are Tibet, Inner Mongolia, Guangxi Zhuang, Ningxia Hui, and Xinjiang Uygur. Finally, China also has two special administrative regions, Macau and Hong Kong.

The next smaller level is made up of divisions similar to U.S. or Canadian counties, and are called counties, prefectures, or municipalities. China has more than three thousand of these. Then there are towns and villages, which have their own local administrators.

The Capital City

The capital city of Beijing means "northern capital." The Mongols made the city the capital in 1279, during the reign of Yuan emperor Kublai Khan. They chose the site in what is now northeastern China because it was halfway between the traditional Mongolian homeland in the north and the productive Chinese farmland in the south.

The city is hot and humid in the summer, often lashed by monsoon rains. Autumns are brief and mild, while winters are dry and windy. Spring is warm and dry, but sometimes strong winds whip up dust storms, making it difficult to see and breathe.

Beijing is a big, bustling city, packed with cars, skyscrapers, and people. Beijing is also the cultural center of China, filled with palaces and temples. The largest of these is the Forbidden City, which served as the home of the Chinese emperors for five hundred years. The Forbidden City was built between 1406 and 1420. During that time, 980 buildings were erected. Today, the Forbidden City contains the largest group of ancient wooden buildings in the world. Other important sites in Beijing include the Temple of Heaven, where emperors once prayed for a good harvest, and the Pagoda of Tianning Temple (below).

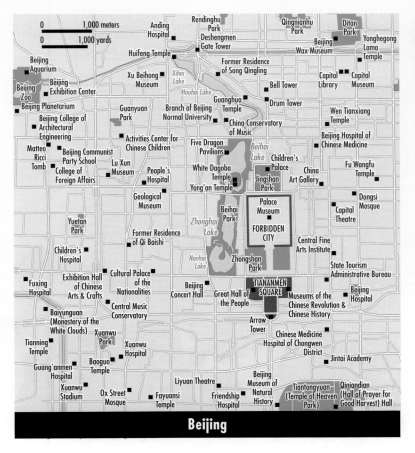

China is ruled by the Communist Party of China (CPC). It is one of the few Communist nations in the world, along with Cuba, North Korea, and Vietnam. Under Communism, people are expected to work for the good of the nation as a whole rather than for their own self-interest. Communist governments typically control a much larger part of people's lives than capitalist nations such as the United States or Canada, where personal freedom is encouraged. In North America, people are free to choose their profession. In China, a profession is sometimes assigned to a person.

The head of the CPC is known as the general secretary. Since the CPC holds virtually all political power, the general secretary is considered the most powerful person in China.

Hu Jintao is both the president of China and the leader of the CPC.

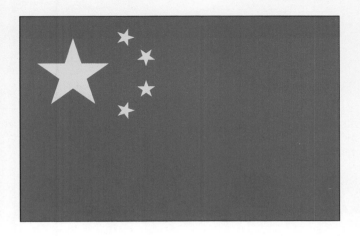

The Flag

China's flag has a simple design. The entire flag is red. In the upper left corner, four small gold stars make a semicircle around one large star. This design carries great symbolism. The red represents the Communist revolution. The large gold star represents the Communist Party, and the smaller stars are the people under its rule. Together, the stars symbolize the unity of the nation. The flag was designed by Zeng Liansong, during a competition following the Communist takeover in 1949.

Constitutionally Speaking

China's current constitution, which was adopted in 1982, lays out the role of the Chinese government and the rights of its citizens. In recent years, the constitution has been amended, or changed, to give citizens a bit more freedom. In 1993, the constitution was changed to limit government control at lower economic levels and provide more opportunity for ordinary people. In 2004, the Chinese government took a step toward true democracy by amending the constitution to protect citizens' private property and acknowledge the importance of human rights. Chinese authorities typically do not enforce these changes, however. For example, the government has jailed journalists who have been critical of its policies, and it has put down the rise of rival political parties. Nevertheless, many see China's recent constitutional additions as a step in the right direction.

The National People's Congress meets in the Great Hall of the People in Beijing.

Parts of the Government

In China, the official head of the executive branch of government is the president. The position of president is largely ceremonial. The president is elected to a five-year term by the National People's Congress (NPC), the lawmaking part of the government, rather than by the people.

Most of the true executive power in China lies with the State Council, also known as the Central People's Government. The head of the State Council is the premier, who also serves for five years. The Chinese president has the power to nominate the State Council's premier, but final approval of the nomination rests within the council itself.

The State Council oversees the operations of the government's many ministries and agencies. Each ministry is responsible for a different aspect of Chinese society, such as finance and justice. The State Council has about forty members. Each is nominated by the premier, but the NPC has the final approval of their appointment.

The NPC is the legislative branch of the Chinese government. It has about three thousand delegates. They are elected by smaller governmental assemblies in the provinces, and the CPC strongly influences the choices. Even so, about a third of the members of the NPC do not belong to the Communist Party.

CHINA'S NATIONAL GOVERNMENT

Executive Branch

PRESIDENT

STATE COUNCIL

PREMIER

MINISTERS

Legislative Branch

NATIONAL PEOPLE'S CONGRESS

Judicial Branch

SUPREME PEOPLE'S COURT

LOCAL PEOPLE'S COURT

The members of the National People's Congress serve five-year terms.

The Supreme People's Court building is in Beijing. It is the highest court in China.

With so many members, it's hard for the NPC to get much done. For a group of this size, meaningful debate over important matters is almost impossible. The NPC meets only once a year for about a month. A smaller version of the NPC, with just 150 members, meets regularly. It is called the Standing Committee. The Standing Committee handles day-to-day duties and can vote on matters ranging from the approval of new laws to issues involving other countries.

China's judicial branch assures that laws are obeyed and punishes those who break them. The highest court in the land is called the Supreme People's Court, which tries important cases and reviews decisions made by other courts. The Supreme People's Court has more than three hundred judges. On all court levels, the CPC heavily influences the appointment of judges, so cases can also be influenced. And while China technically assures all people a proper legal defense, this does not always happen. Similarly, some people in power can, by Chinese law, keep people in prison for years without a trial. Such abuses have become less common in recent years, however. This may be because the number of private lawyers who are not members of the CPC is rising, and some are willing to fight for basic civil rights.

Justices from the Supreme People's Court at a meeting with justices of high courts of neighboring nations. Chinese courts have sometimes been described as unfair and abusive to people accused of crimes.

National Anthem

"March of the Volunteers," China's national anthem, was originally written for a 1935 film called *Sons and Daughters of the Storm*. Tian Han wrote the words, and Nie Er composed the music. It was adopted as the national anthem in 1949, when the Communists gained control of the country.

Arise, you who don't want to be slaves
Using our flesh and blood, we shall build
  a new Great Wall
The Chinese nation is facing the gravest danger of all
In urgency, everyone cries out the last call
Arise! Arise! Arise! We will be united as one!
Brave the enemy's artillery, march on!
Brave the enemy's artillery, march on!
March on!
March on!

Fighting Forces

China has the largest standing army in the world, with more than two million soldiers. The military, known as the People's Liberation Army (PLA), includes an army, a navy, and an air force. The PLA is under the direction of the CPC. For the most part, the PLA is a defensive force, used to protect the nation's borders and keep the peace among its population. But China is one of the few countries in the world with nuclear weapons.

Foreign Affairs

China's relationship with other nations varies tremendously, and these relationships have changed a lot over the years. There was a great deal of tension between China and the United States following World War II and Mao Zedong's establishment of the People's Republic of China. At the time, the United States chose to recognize Chiang Kai-shek's government in Taiwan as China's true leadership.

The relationship between China and the United States improved dramatically following a visit to China by U.S. president Richard M. Nixon in 1972. Since then, the two nations have had a relatively friendly relationship. And although it may seem strange that a Communist nation like China can get

along with a capitalist nation like the United States, American influence has played a role in moving China toward greater respect for the rights of its people.

In 1972, U.S. president Richard Nixon visited China and met with Mao Zedong (right). The visit greatly improved relations between the two countries.

CHAPTER SIX

A Blooming Economy

I N TERMS OF SHEER SIZE, CHINA'S ECONOMY IS A MONSTER. It is, in fact, the second-largest economy in the world after the United States. Since the 1980s, the Chinese economy has grown at an average rate of about 10 percent per year, the biggest growth of any country in the world. It is the world's largest exporter, which means it sells more goods to other countries than any other nation in the world. China's gross domestic product, or GDP—the total value of all goods and services produced—was nearly six trillion dollars in 2010.

China's economy was not always so robust. In the years following the Communist victory in the late 1940s, the Chinese economy was sluggish. This led to some of the worst human suffering in history. The country could not grow enough food, and millions of people died of starvation. Reform programs launched in the late 1970s helped improve the economy.

Opposite: **A lush field of rice. China produces more rice than any other country in the world.**

The Chinese Economy

The guiding principle of China's economy is state capitalism. Although it is in some ways similar to the capitalist economies of the United States and Canada, the government closely manages the Chinese economy. In the United States, the government regulates certain industries, but mostly, American businesses can do as they wish. In China, the larger businesses have remained under full government control; medium and small businesses have a mix of government and private ownership.

A Little History

Following the establishment of Communist rule, the Chinese government took over the administration of all aspects of the

A woman sells her goods at a vegetable market.

Chinese currency is called renminbi ("people's money"). The basic unit of currency is the yuan. A fen is one-hundredth of a yuan, and a jiao is one-tenth of a yuan. Paper bills come in values of 1, 10, 20, 50, and 100 yuan, and 1, 2, and 5 jiao. Coins come in values of 1 yuan, 1 and 5 jiao, and 1, 2, and 5 fen.

Chinese money is colorful and intricately designed. China's standard bills feature former leader Mao Zedong on the front and famous landmarks on the back. For example, the 10-yuan bill shows the Three Gorges of the Yangtze River, and the 100-yuan bill shows the Great Hall of the People in Beijing. In 2011, 6.5 yuan equaled one U.S. dollar.

economy. If something played a role in the nation's finances, the government took control. This is known as a planned economy. At the time, China was still mostly a nation of farmers. The CPC wanted to move people off the land and into industry.

China successfully increased its manufacturing, but with tragic side effects. With fewer farmers, there was less food. There was also destructive flooding. These two things caused widespread famine. Historians now believe twenty to forty million people starved to death between 1958 and 1961. This caused not just further economic difficulties but general bitterness and unrest among the Chinese people. By the time of Mao Zedong's death in 1976, it became clear that serious changes were needed.

How Many Chi in a Li?

Internationally, the Chinese follow the metric system. Distances are measured in meters, weight in kilograms, and so on. But within their nation, the Chinese have a system of weights and measures that is all their own.

Distance is measured in chi and li. One chi equals 1.175 feet (0.36 m), while 1 li is about 0.3 miles (0.5 km). The basic unit of weight is the jin, which equals about 1 pound (0.5 kg).

These changes were led by Communist leader Deng Xiaoping. He moved China away from the planned economy by gradually allowing more capitalist elements. He believed that if citizens were given more opportunity for personal success, they would be more productive. This would lead the nation to increased growth. After the Communist revolution,

Workers at a glassware factory in 1973. At the time, the government was in control of all factories in China.

the government took land away from farmers so it could be used on behalf of the nation as a whole. To encourage people to work harder and grow more, the government gave land back to farmers in the late 1970s and early 1980s.

Then the government began permitting more foreign investment. People from other nations were allowed to put their money into China's future. This allowed the Chinese to build more factories, buy more raw materials, and upgrade out-dated equipment. Also, more ordinary citizens were allowed

Workers make dolls at a toy factory in Guangdong Province on the southeast coast. In 2010, China was the world's largest exporter.

Hong Kong is one of the wealthiest areas of China. It is a world center of banking.

to pursue private business interests for the first time. As the years went on, the CPC allowed private citizens and foreign companies to become key decision makers in some of the nation's larger industries. It also relaxed many laws and regulations. It still, however, kept a fairly tight rein on the most important businesses, such as banking and oil. As a result of these changes, China has experienced one of the most rapid economic expansions in history. Poverty levels have dropped, and the standard of living has risen. The nation is now one of the greatest economic forces in the world.

He'll Drink to That

Zong Qinghou, one of China's wealthiest men, was born in 1945 to a family of modest means. He did not attend either high school or college, and his lack of education made it hard for him to find a job that paid well. Then, in the late 1980s, he took over a small company called Wahaha, which produces nutritious drinks for children. He expanded the product line and then entered into a partnership with French company Danone in 1996. By the 2000s, Zong was one of China's few billionaires.

There have been a few negative effects of the economic changes in China. Prices have increased. During the planned economy, just about everyone had a job. But now, if a business is not doing well, people might lose their jobs. Other people

In Chinese cities, people often shop in large supermarkets.

A worker puts the finishing touches on a taxi at a car factory in Shanghai.

can only find part-time work, so they do not make as much money as they need. Despite these problems, many people believe that the nation is heading in the right direction.

Manufacturing and Mining

China makes nearly 10 percent of all the manufactured goods in the world. It makes consumer products such as shoes, clothing, toys, radios, televisions, computers, and cell phones. It produces machinery, weapons, cars, and trucks. It supplies huge amounts of iron, steel, tin, nickel, antimony, tungsten, zinc, manganese, bauxite, gypsum, silver, and gold. China is, in fact, among the most mineral-rich of all nations. It is also a huge producer of coal and a steady supplier of oil and natural gas.

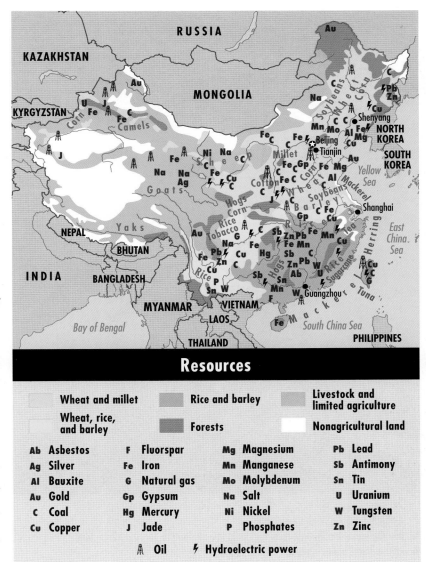

Resources

Wheat and millet	Rice and barley	Livestock and limited agriculture
Wheat, rice, and barley	Forests	Nonagricultural land

Ab	Asbestos	F	Fluorspar	Mg	Magnesium	Pb	Lead
Ag	Silver	Fe	Iron	Mn	Manganese	Sb	Antimony
Al	Bauxite	G	Natural gas	Mo	Molybdenum	Sn	Tin
Au	Gold	Gp	Gypsum	Na	Salt	U	Uranium
C	Coal	Hg	Mercury	Ni	Nickel	W	Tungsten
Cu	Copper	J	Jade	P	Phosphates	Zn	Zinc

⚒ Oil   ⚡ Hydroelectric power

Services

In service industries, people provide a service for someone rather than making or growing a product. Doctors, bankers, cooks, and garbage collectors all work in service industries. China's service industries have grown fast in recent years. Shopping malls, restaurants, hotels, hair salons, and real estate agencies have sprouted across the land. Service industries employ more than one-third of China's workforce. As China's economy continues to grow, ordinary

As the Chinese economy has expanded in recent years, many malls have been built to accommodate the growing number of citizens who have extra income.

Chinese will have money to spend. This should help stores that sell everything from clothing to computers to lawn mowers.

Tourism is an important service industry. In recent years, China has lured more and more travelers looking for new destinations. Nearly fifty-six million foreigners traveled to China in 2010, making it the third most visited country in the world. All those travelers spend money on restaurants and hotels, tour guides and taxi drivers, helping boost China's economy.

Agriculture

Agriculture was once the center of China's economy, but it now makes up less than 15 percent of the nation's GDP. Nevertheless, China is the largest producer of agricultural products in the world. The nation produces huge amounts of wheat and rice, along with potatoes, sorghum, peanuts, millet, tea, soybeans, barley, corn, cotton, and tobacco. China's farmers also produce chicken, eggs, and pork.

What China Grows, Makes, and Mines

Agriculture (2007)

Rice	185,490,000 metric tons
Corn	151,830,000 metric tons
Wheat	109,850,000 metric tons

Manufacturing (2009 exports, value in U.S dollars)

Electrical machinery	$301,100,000,000
Power generation equipment	$236,000,000,000
Clothing	$100,500,000,000

Mining

Coal (2008)	2,720,000,000 metric tons
Oil (2009)	1,383,000,000 barrels
Iron (2008)	270,000,000 metric tons

A Sea of People

CHINA IS THE MOST POPULATED NATION ON EARTH, with more than 1.3 billion citizens. That's roughly one-fifth of all the humans in the world. China has been the most populous nation for centuries. Most Chinese live in the eastern third of the nation, either in fertile farmlands or in heavily industrialized areas. To the west, the population drops. It is thinnest in the extreme west and some north-central regions. No one at all lives in the harshest deserts and mountains.

Opposite: **More than 160 cities in China have populations of more than one million people.**

Crowd Control

With so many people in one country, some problems arise. At times, China has experienced severe food shortages. People there worried about the cost of educating all the children or whether there would be enough jobs for them. In the early 1970s, women were still having an average of about five children each. This meant the population would continue to grow at an alarming rate, which could lead the nation to great hardships.

In 1979, the government began a new program that was both highly controversial and highly effective: the one-child

Population of Major Cities

Shanghai	18 million
Beijing	13.2 million
Guangzhou	12 million
Shenzhen	8.6 million
Tianjin	8.2 million
Chongqing	7.5 million
Hong Kong	7 million
Dongguan	7 million
Nanjing	6.8 million
Wuhan	6.6 million

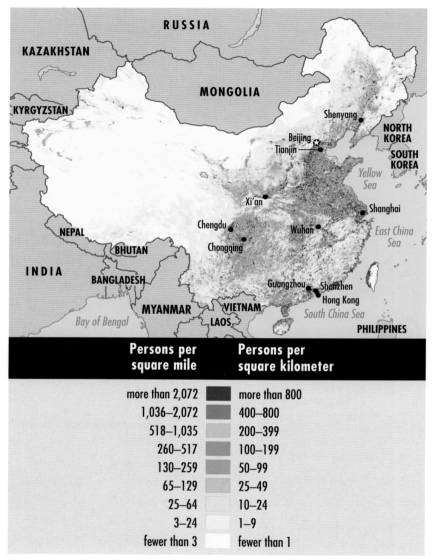

Persons per square mile		Persons per square kilometer
more than 2,072		more than 800
1,036–2,072		400–800
518–1,035		200–399
260–517		100–199
130–259		50–99
65–129		25–49
25–64		10–24
3–24		1–9
fewer than 3		fewer than 1

policy. Put simply, it bars most couples from having more than one child. Couples who have more than one child are fined. Some people say the rule is extreme. But roughly three-quarters of the Chinese population supports the plan, and the birth rate in China now ranks among the lowest in the world. Between 1979, when the program began, and the year 2000, it has been estimated that more than 250 million births that might have occurred were avoided.

Chinese children are under tremendous pressure to succeed in school and later in their careers. This is because they will be expected to care for all of their aging relatives when they reach adulthood. Before the one-child policy, this burden was shared by a group of siblings, but now it falls on just one child.

Missing Girls

Many Chinese families prefer boys to girls because boys can carry on the family name and are thought to be better able to take care of their aging parents. Since the one-child policy was put in place, some women now have abortions after finding out they are going to have a girl. Many female babies are also given up for adoption. By 2005, there were 120 boys born for every 100 girls. When these boys grow up, they may not be able to find wives.

The Chinese Melting Pot

China has fifty-six officially recognized ethnic groups. The largest is the Han, who make up roughly 91 percent of the population. Their ancestry in China dates back thousands of years. The name Han comes from the Han dynasty (206 BCE– 220 CE), one of the most celebrated periods in the nation's history. It was a time of peace and prosperity, of cultural richness and social unity. People shared a common written language, a common devotion to the values of Confucianism, and a general feeling of optimism.

Locations of Ethnic Groups

Dai	
Han (Chinese)	
Indonesian	
Korean	
Miao-Yao	
Mongolian	
Mon-Khmer	
Tajik	
Tibeto-Burman	
Tungusic	
Turkic	
Uninhabited	

Populations of Ethnic Groups

Han	1.21 billion
Zhuang	18 million
Uyghur	11.25 million
Manchu	10.5 million
Hui	10 million
Miao	8 million
Yi	7 million
Tujia	5.75 million
Mongol	5 million
Tibetan	5 million

Over time, the Han acquired more land and expanded their territory. Any non-Han groups they encountered either joined their ranks or were forced out. Today, the Han are the dominant group throughout eastern and central China. They are also the overwhelming majority in Hong Kong and Macau.

The remaining fifty-five ethnic groups make up about 8 percent of China's population, or roughly 125 million people. Most of these minorities are distinct from the Han in more than just their ancestry. They have their own spoken and written languages, religious practices, and social values. Although most Chinese minority groups are tiny in comparison to the Han, their numbers are increasing. That is because the government's one-child policy applies only to the Han. People from other ethnic groups are allowed to have more children.

Minority groups tend to live in specific areas, often distant from the Han. The Han dominate the eastern third of the

A Disappearing People

Among the smallest of China's ethnic minority groups is the Nanai of Heilongjiang Province in the extreme northeast. The people of this group long ago settled along the Ussuri River and survived primarily by fishing. They used dried fish skins to make clothing, which earned them the name Yupi Dazi (fish skin). Early Nanai were also capable farmers, growing fruits and vegetables. They built homes either as cone-shaped tents or round huts, and learned to weave useful items such as baskets. The population of Nanai in China was never large, and World War II took a heavy toll on them. By the time Mao Zedong's Communists took control of China in 1949, only about 300 remained. Today, this nation of 1.3 billion people is home to only about 4,300 Nanai.

country, while minorities are commonly found in outlying regions and frontier territories. Tibetans live in the extreme southwest, for example, while Mongolians live in the north.

Last Name First

In China, a person's family name comes first and the given name comes second. If Michael Jones was a Chinese name, it would be written Jones Michael. He would be called Mr. Jones, though, not Mr. Michael, and never just Jones. In China, people always use a title, such as Mr. or Ms., or a professional term like Teacher or Doctor. The Chinese rarely call someone solely by a given name. Instead of saying, "Hello, Michael," they would say, "Hello, Jones Michael." The one exception is when a parent is speaking to a child.

More than three hundred languages are used in China. The most common one is simply called Chinese. It is one of the oldest languages in the world still in active use. It has many different dialects (variations), and the one that is the official language of the nation is called Mandarin. Mandarin itself is made up of a cluster of dialects. The one spoken in Beijing is considered the national language. This version is also called Putonghua, which means "common speech."

A Chinese boy carefully makes a sign. Writing is considered an art form in China.

Dialects can differ from each other in many ways. They might use different vocabulary. In Chinese, the tone that a person uses when speaking a word can change the word's meaning. So, whether words or phrases are said with a high or low tone, or a rising or falling tone might also vary from dialect to dialect. These details are crucial to the meaning,

China has a high literacy rate. More than 99 percent of the people younger than age twenty-five can read and write.

It takes a lot of practice to learn to write Chinese characters.

and some dialects are so different from one another that two people may not realize they are using the same language. Some other common Chinese dialects are Cantonese (used in Hong Kong and Macau), Hakka, and Wu.

Words on Loan

Loan words are words that are borrowed from one language for use in another. They are often altered slightly to better fit the second language. A few Chinese words have made their way into English. Here are some you might know:

chow	a casual term for food, probably from a Cantonese word referring to cooking		ketchup	probably Cantonese in origin, referring to juice or sauce made from tomatoes
gung ho	extremely enthusiastic, from the Mandarin phrase *gongye hezhuoshe*, which refers to people working together to achieve a common objective		silk	rooted in the Chinese word *si*
			tea	from the Chinese dialect called Amoy
			tycoon	a businessperson of great wealth, from the Chinese term for a man of great social standing or power

The written Chinese language does not have an alphabet. Instead, it is a collection of more than fifty thousand symbols and characters. Only about five thousand of the characters are used in everyday life. Each character represents a word or a part of a word. Some characters are simplified versions of familiar objects. Other characters represent abstract concepts. Sometimes a character has more than one meaning, with each having little or nothing to do with the others. In this case, additional characters or markings are included. In the 1950s, the Chinese government tried to promote literacy, or the ability to read and write, among citizens. As part of this effort, the government led a crusade to create a standard written language. Many characters were made simpler so they would require as few line strokes as possible. Today, written communication within the country is more efficient than ever.

Complex Beliefs

M OST CHINESE PEOPLE VIEW RELIGION A BIT differently than people typically do in the United States and Canada. In North America, people might consider themselves Christian, or Jewish, or Muslim. They might read certain holy books and worship in specific places like a church, a synagogue, or a mosque.

The majority of Chinese do not consider themselves religious. But even among those who do have beliefs, religion is not always the correct word. Instead, they may follow a specific philosophy or have a particular way of thinking, but they do not honor one god or attend religious services. Chinese people often take bits and pieces from different religions, while also bringing in ideas from Chinese legends and folklore. Many also have a deep respect for the natural world, the spirits of their ancestors, a variety of heroes and gods, and unseen forces in the universe. Each person, therefore, ends up with his or her own set of beliefs.

Opposite: **People pray at the Confucius Temple in Nanjing. Confucius thought that rulers should set a moral example for people to follow.**

A Catholic priest leads a service in Beijing. China is home to an estimated ten to fifteen million Catholics.

The Big Three

Three main religions, or schools of thought, are practiced in China today. One is known as Daoism. It is based on the idea that the universe has a natural flow to it, and that a person can find inner peace by finding his or her place within that flow. Daoists refer to this flow as the *dao*, and the energy of the dao as the *de*. The de is made up of forces both negative (the yin) and positive (the yang). The yin and yang must be present in order to maintain a balance and achieve completeness.

Church and State

For centuries, people in China had observed religious practices of one kind or another. Then, following the establishment of the People's Republic of China in 1949, all religious activities were banned. The government took control of churches, temples, pagodas, mosques, and schools of spirituality, and used them for new purposes. Religious leaders were forced to find new professions. Many governments around the world urged China to reconsider. In 1978, the Chinese government gradually began to allow some religious activity. When the Chinese constitution was revised in 1982, the government granted people the right to observe whatever religion they wanted. Today, the CPC is more tolerant of religious worship than ever before.

Because people are part of the universe, they are part of the dao. A person finds his ideal place within the dao when calm and restful. Aggressive behavior puts a person at odds with nature. Also included in Daoism is a reverence for the natural world and respect for one's ancestors, who continue to exist after death without bodily form. Daoism began as an important school of philosophy with Laozi in the sixth century BCE.

Another major Chinese school of thought is called Confucianism. It began with the philosopher Confucius, who lived around the same time as Laozi. Some people say he witnessed war and suffering and became convinced that society

Laozi is usually considered the founder of Daoism.

Incense smoke fills the air at a Daoist temple.

was headed on a path to destruction. He came to believe that each individual had a duty to act in an ethical manner, and that this would lead to a well-ordered society. This belief system, built on a code of commonsense morality, included respectable public conduct, a willingness to help others, the ability to think for oneself, fairness and balance in all relationships, and the practice of constant and honest self-evaluation.

Some people consider Confucianism a religion. Others do not because it does not worship any type of god, does not have

The Wisdom of Confucius

Confucius was renowned for his commonsense wisdom. Here are some of his most famous statements, although no one knows for sure whether he said them:

Everything has its beauty, but not everyone sees it.
Before you embark on a journey of revenge, dig two graves.
It does not matter how slowly you go, so long as you do not stop.
Respect yourself and others will respect you.
Wheresoever you go, go with all your heart.
Have no friends not equal to yourself.
Hold faithfulness and sincerity as first principles.

any sort of priest or minister, and does not address the issue of life after death. Despite this, the Chinese government has increasingly recognized Confucianism as an official system of beliefs.

Performers work in an ancient movement style for a ceremony marking Confucius's birthday.

Visitors climb a giant statue of the Buddha in Hong Kong. About 90 percent of the people in Hong Kong practice Buddhism, often combined with some other religion.

Buddhism is the other major religion practiced in China. It is one of the largest religions in the world, with more than 350 million followers. Buddhism began in India with the teachings of a prince named Siddhartha Gautama. Born sometime in the 500s or 400s BCE, Gautama was a member of a

The Niujie Mosque, the largest mosque in China, is in Beijing.

Religions in China

It is impossible to get reliable information about how many people follow different religions in China. Many people observe practices from more than one religion, and some religions are considered more a collection of ideas than actual faiths. In recent years, the Chinese government has allowed more religious freedom. Because of this, religious trends have changed rapidly. Many people who in earlier years claimed to be nonreligious may, in fact, have long been devoted followers of a specific faith. Here is one estimate of the percentages of Chinese who follow different religions.

Religion	Percentage
No religion	60%
Daoism	25%
Confucianism	22%
Buddhism	20%
Christianity	5%
Islam	2%
Judaism	less than 1%

Siddhartha Gautama spent years meditating, until he believed he understood why people suffer. After that he became known as the Buddha, which means "the Enlightened One."

wealthy family. In his late twenties, he rejected his privileged life and set out to find true happiness and contentment. He traveled throughout northern India. He practiced meditation and finally felt he had come to understand human suffering. His teachings are called the dharma.

The Buddhist dharma states that humans are reborn after they die. If people did good things in past lives, then their

Li Hongzhi and the Falun Gong Movement

As the Chinese government has permitted greater religious freedom in recent years, new forms of worship have evolved. One of these is the Falun Gong, or Falun Dafa, movement. Its creator, Li Hongzhi, first revealed it to the public in 1992. Like so many other religious practices in China, Falun Gong gathered ideas and beliefs from a variety of other religions and philosophies. The main features are attention to moral behavior, particularly honesty, compassion, and patience, and a series of slow-moving exercises. The movement experienced enormous popularity in the 1990s. The CPC was at first tolerant of the Falun Gong movement. But then, in 1999, more than one hundred thousand followers gathered in Tiananmen Square in Beijing. The government became alarmed because it had no prior knowledge of the event. Although the protest was peaceful, the CPC banned Falun Gong later that year.

present lives will be mostly enjoyable. If people did bad things, then their present lives will be unpleasant. From this comes the concept of good and bad karma. According to the dharma, people can free themselves from this trap. They can achieve inner peace, or nirvana, by giving up all cravings for money, power, and worldly goods. Gautama's followers later called him the Buddha, meaning "Enlightened One."

Chinese opera tells stories that have been passed down through the centuries.

Storytime

Chinese myths, legends, and folklore often tell of past events that occurred long ago. Some are a mix of fact and fiction. Others are pure fantasy, similar to fairy tales. These stories were created to teach, inspire, and entertain. Common themes in these tales include creation of the universe, of the world, and of China. Other tales are about heroes, both real and unreal, important events in Chinese history, and the importance of good morals and social values. It is believed that the earliest mythological stories appeared in China, in both written and oral form, around the twelfth century BCE. As the centuries passed, they were turned into other artistic forms, such as theater, dance, music, and poetry.

All Creatures Great and Small

Chinese mythology features a broad array of characters. Each possesses a specific power over the forces of the universe. For example, Lei Gong is China's god of thunder, and Guan Yu is the god of war. Chinese mythology also includes many fantastic beasts. There is Bashe, a giant snake that ate elephants, and Jiufeng, a nine-headed bird that killed people by absorbing their spirits. One of the best-known mythological Chinese creatures is the dragon. Although in other cultures dragons are often portrayed negatively, in China they are revered as a symbol of strength and achievement. A person who accomplishes great things or has a high standing in society is often compared to a dragon. In Chinese mythology, dragons are often associated with water, and farmers often pray to dragons for rain during times of drought.

Rich Traditions

THE CHINESE HAVE ALWAYS BEEN CREATORS, AND THEIR inventions and art stretch back as far as the history of the nation itself. Through their innovations, the Chinese have given much to the rest of the world.

Opposite: **Chinese art often depicts nature.**

The Written Word

One of the most important Chinese inventions was paper, which was first made more than two thousand years ago. The Chinese also invented movable type, which launched the first system of printing. Movable type enabled the Chinese to create books in large numbers. This made it more likely that many of their important works would survive through the ages. Chinese writers produced some of the earliest literary classics, including the *I Ching*, a book that focuses on gaining greater insight into the balance between the yin and the yang and the universe. The Chinese also wrote many of the first poetry collections, the first dictionary and encyclopedia, and original and innovative forms of both the novel and the short story.

The Poetry of Wang Wei

Wang Wei is one of China's most beloved poets, painters, and musicians. Born in 699 to a prominent family, he became one of the most influential artists of the Tang dynasty. One of his most frequent subjects was the natural world. Sadly, none of his original paintings have survived to this day, although artists he influenced have re-created several. Many of his poems, however, were published. Some are still enormously popular today. The following is an English translation of one of his best-loved poems, "Returning to Songshan Mountain."

The limpid river runs between the bushes
The horse and cart are moving idly on
The water flows as if with a mind of its own
At dusk, the birds return to perch together
The desolate town is faced by an ancient ferry
The setting sun now fills the autumn hills
And far below high Songshan's tumbling ridges
Returning home, I close the door for now

Beginning in the late 1940s, after the Communists took control of China, all literature had to serve the goals and objectives of the government. That meant that most literature was propaganda—material promoting the strengths of one political point of view while condemning all others. In the late 1970s, the Chinese government relaxed this policy, and Chinese literature and other art forms began to flourish again. Allowed even greater artistic freedom in the 1980s, writers began to use many different forms, from poetry to drama, to criticize the government.

Today, China publishes more printed literature than any other nation. In part, this is because of its huge population, the improvement of the literacy rate in recent years, and the demand from Chinese people who live abroad. Commercial literature is still controlled by the Communist Party of China (CPC), which issues licenses to all publishing houses and can revoke them at any time. The CPC also retains the power

to edit, censor, and in some cases deny the publication of any book. China has thousands of "pirate" publishers, printing books and magazines that have no chance of receiving government approval. Online publishing has also become a favored channel among these cultural rebels, as the government has great difficulty policing the Internet.

Book publishing has been growing in China in recent years. In 2007, nearly a quarter million different books were published there.

Visual Arts

The Chinese have worked in various visual art forms—paintings, sculpture, pottery—for thousands of years. Early works focused on everyday things, such as animals and people. They

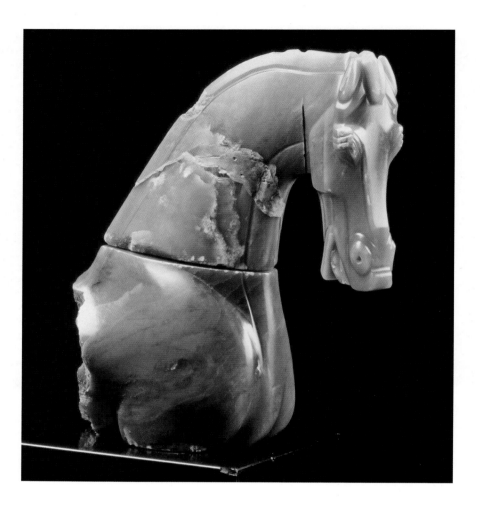

This jade head of a horse dates back about two thousand years, to the Han dynasty.

later evolved into more abstract designs. Eventually, there was a focus on landscapes.

Sculptors began with clay and common stone but soon turned to more dramatic material such as bronze and jade. Jade is a beautiful greenish stone that has become closely associated with Chinese art. For potters, porcelain was the medium of choice.

The National Art Museum of China

One of China's most impressive collections of art is in the National Art Museum. Located in the capital city of Beijing, it houses tens of thousands of paintings, prints, cartoons, puppets, kites, sculptures, costumes, and other items. The museum displays work from Chinese artists present and past, as well as artists from Western cultures. More than a million people visit the museum each year.

The most revered traditional art form in China is calligraphy. Calligraphy is the art of making the written language beautiful. Chinese characters are visually interesting, and calligraphy attempts to make them even more so. In ancient times, calligraphy was done with the finest inks on the finest silk. It was then hung in homes with the same appreciation given to treasured paintings. Calligraphy is still widely practiced today.

A man does calligraphy on a sidewalk in Beijing.

Gong Li helped popularize Chinese movies in the West.

Much of China's modern visual art is influenced by European and American styles. Artists continue to make use of traditional Chinese subjects—the natural world, the people around them, the country's many breathtaking landforms. Today, they often portray these subjects using striking colors and aggressive designs.

Film has become an important Chinese art form in recent decades. Directors such as Zhang Yimou and Chen Kaige have made moving and visually stunning films such as *Raise the Red Lantern*, *The Story of Qiu Ju*, and *Life on a String*. Many of these films have starred Gong Li, the Chinese actress best known by the Western world.

Music

Music is an important part of the Chinese heritage. Traditional Chinese music features many instruments that are rarely heard in the Western world. Common percussion instruments include gongs, bells, cymbals, and tuned drums. In the woodwind family there are flutes such as the *dizi*, and several types of panpipes such as the *sheng*. Stringed instruments are often plucked, bowed, or struck rather than strummed. They include the *erhu*, a two-string fiddle played with a bow, and the *guqin*, a zitherlike instrument that sits on a table or a lap. The music is often spare and has sudden shifts in tempo. To the Chinese people, there is always great depth and meaning.

The seated children are playing the erhu. Its origins in China date back a thousand years.

Chinese opera involves carefully choreographed movements and elaborate costumes.

One renowned form of Chinese music is opera. The Chinese have been composing opera since the third century CE. Probably the best-known troupe is the Beijing Opera, celebrated for its colorful costumes and makeup. The Beijing Opera mixes music, singing, speaking, dancing, and acrobatics to tell stories that are often based on centuries-old folktales and legends. Every movement the performers make has significance, and the precise manner in which they execute each one takes years to master.

As with so many other art forms, the Communist government changed music following its seizure of power in the late 1940s. The new rulers insisted that the themes and subjects of all new compositions had to further government objectives. As a result, songwriters produced songs that promoted national pride or focused on the struggles of the Communist revolution. These latter songs were often heavily orchestrated and dramatic. As government control relaxed in the late 1970s and early 1980s, a very different music scene began to evolve. Today, following decades of foreign influence, Chinese music is a mix of traditional flavors and modern style. China's youth retains an appreciation for the music of its nation's past, while also embracing everything from hard rock and heavy metal to mainstream pop, hip-hop, and Mandarin-language rap.

Rock, hip-hop, and other types of modern music have become much more popular in China in the twenty-first century.

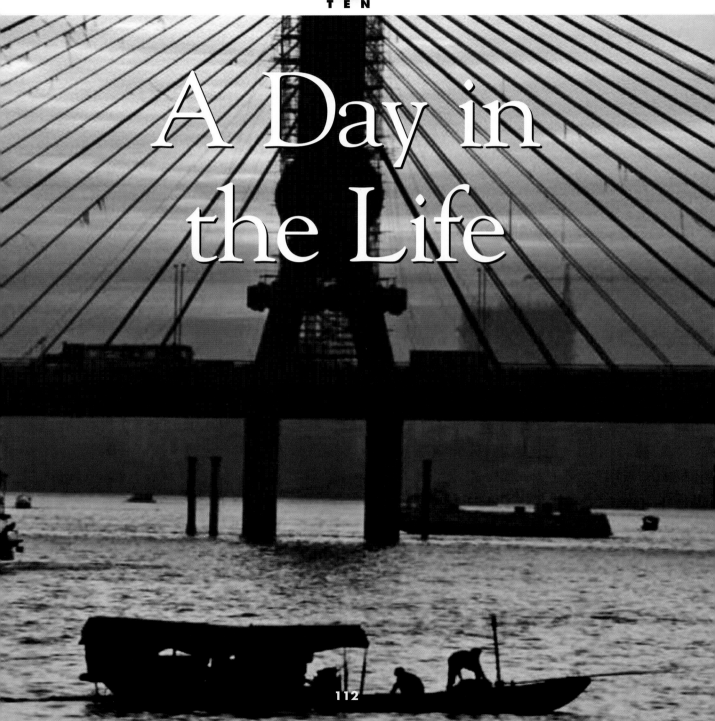

A Day in
the Life

112

CHINESE PEOPLE TEND TO LEAD BUSY LIVES. THEY GET up early, go to school or work, come home for dinner, and relax before going to bed. Weekends are for spending time with family, doing chores, running errands, and getting some much-needed rest. Regardless of where a Chinese person lives, whether it be in a bustling city or farming district, there is always plenty to be done.

Opposite: **Many people working on the Pearl River in southern China start their day before sunrise.**

A New Day Dawns

Most Chinese do not sleep late. They get up with the sunrise, shower and dress, and sit down to breakfast. Another important part of the morning ritual is exercise. The Chinese place a high value on health, and most people exercise for about fifteen to thirty minutes in the morning. Some do this in their homes, and some join others at a local park as part of a group workout. The Chinese learned long ago that exercise is a crucial part of each day's preparation. It helps to keep one's focus sharp, increases energy and stamina, and contributes to a person's overall well-being, not just of the body but also the mind and spirit.

Chinese people typically eat with chopsticks.

Chinese food is popular around the world because of its variety and delicious flavors. Most food in China is eaten either with rice or noodles. Tofu, which is made from soy, is often eaten instead of meat, because it offers many of the same nutrients, but is healthier and less expensive. The Chinese also eat many kinds of vegetables, ranging from broccoli and carrots to bamboo shoots and bok choy. Common meats include beef, chicken, pork, and duck. Fish and shellfish are also common.

The method in which a Chinese meal is prepared varies tremendously depending on the region. Each region has developed its own style. In northern China, noodles are generally favored over rice. In the south, the opposite holds true. In Sichuan Province, in south-central China, cooks use many spices and peppers, so the food is often quite hot. Beijing is home to some of the tastiest roast duck in the world.

Food in China is typically eaten using chopsticks. Sometimes Chinese may need a spoon or fork, but using a knife at a meal is rare. Knives are considered kitchen tools, used for preparing a meal, not eating it. Most foods are cut in bite-size pieces so they can easily be picked up with chopsticks. Chopped-up items also cook faster, so they take less time to prepare.

Tea Time

Tea is a favorite drink of almost all Chinese people. According to legend, it was accidentally discovered by the Chinese emperor, Shen Nong, nearly five thousand years ago. Supposedly, the emperor settled down beneath a tea bush to enjoy a cup of boiled water, and one of the leaves broke away and drifted into his cup.

The Chinese enjoy tea any time of day. They rarely add honey, milk, or sugar to their tea, as people do in the West. Tea comes in many varieties, including green tea, black tea, white tea, oolong, and jasmine.

Breakfast in China

Chinese people eat many different foods for breakfast. For a quick start, people often eat bread and yogurt. People with a little more time might make congee (right), a watery dish of boiled rice. Many Chinese enjoy crullers—fried dough that is usually rolled into sticks. Another breakfast food is *zongzi*, balls of sticky rice wrapped in reeds or bamboo leaves, and flavored with bean paste, ham, or pork. Tea and soy milk are common drinks to begin the day.

Schooltime

Chinese students usually begin classes around 8:30 in the morning each day. They study subjects such as math, science, history, computers, physical education, art, music, grammar, and reading. Although Chinese is the primary language taught, students also learn a second language, often English. In the middle of the day, students have lunch and a short recess period. Classes last a bit longer in China than in the United States or Canada. The school day usually continues until around 4:00 or 4:30 in the afternoon. It is also common for school to be held six days a week rather than five.

Education is highly valued in China, and children are expected to work hard and do their best. Competition to get into the best colleges is fierce and begins early, even as early as preschool. Children begin taking important exams from age five or six. Exams play a huge role in determining a child's future. A student that does well may go on to an excellent college and a brilliant career. Those who do not do well on exams may have to settle for a less prestigious school or work at a low-paying job for the rest of their lives.

Most students in Hong Kong wear uniforms.

National Holidays

New Year's Day	January 1
Spring Festival/Chinese New Year	Late January or early February
Qingming Festival	April 4 or 5
May Day	May 1
Dragon Boat Festival	Usually early to mid-June
Mid-Autumn Festival	Usually in September
National Day	October 1

An elderly woman sits with a young child. About 9 percent of the people in China are sixty-five and older.

All in the Family

The family unit is one of the most important building blocks in Chinese society. And, as with so many other aspects of the culture, the family structure is usually clear-cut and well ordered. Traditionally, the father is considered the highest authority. He is most often the sole breadwinner and has the final say on important matters. When a woman marries she becomes not only a wife but also a daughter-in-law. A daughter-in-law becomes part of a larger family and must contribute in whatever way is needed. It's like marrying a whole group of people rather than just one person. Since Communist rule began, wives and mothers have played a larger role in decision making. In some cases, even children, particularly older ones, have been permitted to offer their thoughts as well. Family elders, such as grandparents, aunts, and uncles, are regarded with the greatest respect in China, and it is not unusual to find them living with younger family members.

In centuries past, it was a point of great pride for a person to pass down property—from material goods and money to houses and land—to the next generation. This practice was interrupted when the Communists took over in 1949. In more recent times, many families have had their land and other holdings returned to them, so people can once again pass their land to their children when they die.

Many Chinese farmers once again own their own land, which means they will be able to pass it on to their children.

China's first high-speed trains began operating in 2007.

Getting Around

In years past, people in China usually stayed near their hometown or village, simply because they had no easy way to travel. Now, more Chinese people are able to afford cars than ever before. This is increasing the amount of traffic and the amount of pollution in the air. There are also more trains, planes, buses, boats, and taxis. The Chinese government is spending billions of dollars to build new roads, railroads, and airports. China is also increasing its high-speed rail system at an amazing rate. This system carries trains that travel at least 120 miles per hour (200 kph). China now has the largest high-speed rail network of any country in the world.

This rise in modern forms of transportation has caused the slow death of a more traditional form, the rickshaw. A rickshaw is a small carriage-like vehicle set on two wheels. It is pulled by a person who holds on to a pair of long rails attached to the vehicle. Tourists have enjoyed rickshaw rides through the streets of China for centuries. But motorized vehicles now clog these same streets, and few tourists want to breathe in the fumes. Bicycles continue to be popular, however, in part because riders can weave through areas where cars are stuck in traffic.

Rickshaw drivers carry tourists through the streets of China. Chinese people, however, seldom ride in rickshaws.

Children practice on the balance beam at a gymnastics school.

The Sporting Life

Chinese people place great emphasis on physical fitness, and many love sports. Among the favorites are soccer, basketball, volleyball, badminton, and table tennis. Sports that are slightly less popular, but still have a large following, include baseball, boxing, cricket, golf, tennis, figure skating, swimming, and gymnastics. The Chinese people got to show their appreciation for many of these sports when Beijing hosted the 2008 Summer Olympic Games.

A Star on Two Continents

Yao Ming has become one of the biggest stars in professional basketball in recent years. He was born in Shanghai in 1980 and displayed athletic skill at an early age. He made his first mark on the game as a member of the Shanghai Sharks—part of the Chinese Basketball Association—while still in his teens. In 2002, he joined the Houston Rockets of the National Basketball Association (NBA) in the United States. Yao Ming quickly made his mark on the American game. At 7 feet 6 inches (2.3 m) tall, he towers over many other NBA players. He has been repeatedly picked for both the NBA All-Star Game and the All-NBA Team. Yao Ming has also competed on international teams. In 2008, he carried the Olympic torch at the start of the Beijing Games.

Chinese people are also fond of board games, including chess, Chinese chess, mah-jongg, and Go. Although these games don't do anything for physical fitness, they help keep the mind sharp.

Martial arts, or wushu, are among the best-known Chinese sports. Martial arts are graceful and fluid forms of stylized fighting. Many people consider them more of an art form than a sport. Martial arts began more than four thousand years ago as a means of preparing soldiers for hand-to-hand combat, which was common in the age before guns. Mastery required discipline and dedication, peak physical fitness, and a tremendous amount of practice. Today, there are dozens of martial arts forms, each with its own philosophy and fighting style.

Fashion Sense

Many Chinese wear clothing that combines the elegance of the past with the dazzle of the present. Some traditional clothing is strikingly beautiful. In the early twentieth century, women wore *qipao*, a long, tight, one-piece dress. During the same period, men wore long gowns called *changshan*.

Today, Chinese wear clothes similar to those worn by people in Europe and North America. Young people, in particular, follow the latest fashion trends and prefer name brands.

A young girl wears a traditional qipao.

Home Sweet Home

Many Chinese people think of their home as a refuge against the outside world, a place of peace and safety. Most homes are

Playing Stop!

Many people are familiar with Go, a Chinese game that uses tiles on a board. But many Chinese children play a much simpler game called Stop! The game can be played with any number of players. Each person needs just a paper and pencil. Players draw a series of vertical lines to act as columns on the paper. At the top of each column, each writes the names of categories of everyday items, for example animals or furniture. To play, one player slowly recites the letters of the alphabet. When another player says "Stop!" all the players have to fill in a word beginning with that letter for each of the categories. Once everyone is done, players compare their words. Words that no one else wrote have the highest point value (say, one thousand). Words that were written by other players have a lower point value (say, five hundred). At the end of the game—which comes when players don't feel like playing anymore—the player with the most points wins.

kept neat and clean. People believe this is good fortune and drives away negative energy.

Some families in China have pets, although this is a relatively recent development. At the start of Communist rule, people were forbidden to have pets because it was considered an unnecessary luxury. This law is no longer in effect, however, and many middle-class families have dogs, cats, birds, or fish.

When family members arrive home, it is customary for them to remove their shoes and put on a pair of comfortable slippers. Children are expected to do their homework and

People typically take off their shoes before entering a Buddhist temple.

Lu Ban and the Flying Wooden Bird

Lu Ban was a man of many talents. Born in the sixth century BCE, he became accomplished in the fields of carpentry, engineering, military strategy, philosophy, and government. He was also an inventor. One of his most famous creations was the "flying wooden bird"—an object made of wood, cloth, and rope that could be lifted by the wind and would remain airborne for long periods. Sound familiar? Many people believe this "bird" became what is known today as the kite. At the time, it was likely used for military purposes, possibly as a warning device or a rescue signal. To this day, the Chinese are known for their beautiful kites.

then help prepare dinner. Mealtime usually involves everyone sitting around a large table and engaging in lively conversation. In the farmlands, children play games or read in the evenings. In cities, they often talk to their friends on the phone or surf the Internet.

City Life, Country Life

Visiting a rural area in China can be like stepping back in time. Farming is the main source of income. People live in wooden homes that are often two or three stories high. The roads are usually unpaved, and wagons are more common than cars. The people are typically relaxed and friendly, and everyone in a community seems to know everyone else. Rural people eat simple meals, mostly from food they grow. Televisions and other modern conveniences are rare. In the

Chinese countryside, local officials are part of the CPC, but they mostly manage things without much interference.

City life is radically different. The sidewalks are crowded with pedestrians, and the streets are jammed with cars. Lights flash and cars honk. People talk on cell phones or eat as they walk. There is an electric sense of purpose and urgency everywhere. For many people in Chinese cities, age-old traditions have been cast aside and replaced by ambition. Among young married couples, both people have careers. They might live in tiny apartments, but they don't care. They have access to the highest-paying jobs and the newest technologies. They are taking advantage of the opportunity to make an impact on their world.

A businessperson in Shanghai eats lunch while working at his laptop.

Timeline

People's Republic of China History

Chinese make their earliest known examples of art.	ca. 6000 BCE
The first Chinese dynasty, the Xia, forms.	ca. 2000 BCE
Chinese philosopher Confucius is born.	500s BCE
China is united under the Qin dynasty; construction begins on the Great Wall.	221–206 BCE
The Han dynasty begins ruling China.	206 BCE
China breaks apart into smaller kingdoms during the Three Kingdoms period.	220–581 CE
The Tang dynasty begins its rule.	618
Mongol leader Kublai Khan establishes the Yuan dynasty.	1279
The Ming overthrow the Mongols.	1368
The Manchu take power and rule as the Qing dynasty.	1644

World History

ca. 2500 BCE	Egyptians build the pyramids and the Sphinx in Giza.
ca. 563 BCE	The Buddha is born in India.
313 CE	The Roman emperor Constantine legalizes Christianity.
610	The Prophet Muhammad begins preaching a new religion called Islam.
1054	The Eastern (Orthodox) and Western (Roman Catholic) Churches break apart.
1095	The Crusades begin.
1215	King John seals the Magna Carta.
1300s	The Renaissance begins in Italy.
1347	The plague sweeps through Europe.
1453	Ottoman Turks capture Constantinople, conquering the Byzantine Empire.
1492	Columbus arrives in North America.
1500s	Reformers break away from the Catholic Church, and Protestantism is born.
1776	The U.S. Declaration of Independence is signed.
1789	The French Revolution begins.

People's Republic of China History

The Republic of China is founded.	**1912**
The Communist Party of China is established.	**1921**
Nationalists and Communists battle for control of China.	**1946– 1949**
Communist leader Mao Zedong declares the establishment of the People's Republic of China; Chiang Kai-shek's Nationalists flee to Taiwan.	**1949**
Famine results in the death of at least 20 million people.	**1958– 1961**
The Cultural Revolution begins.	**1966**
Mao Zedong dies.	**1976**
China begins allowing more religious and economic freedom.	**Late 1970s**
A new constitution is adopted, giving the Chinese people more rights and privileges.	**1982**
The Chinese army kills hundreds of demonstrators in Tiananmen Square.	**1989**
Beijing hosts the Summer Olympics.	**2008**

World History

1865	The American Civil War ends.
1879	The first practical lightbulb is invented.
1914	World War I begins.
1917	The Bolshevik Revolution brings communism to Russia.
1929	A worldwide economic depression begins.
1939	World War II begins.
1945	World War II ends.
1957	The Vietnam War begins.
1969	Humans land on the moon.
1975	The Vietnam War ends.
1989	The Berlin Wall is torn down as communism crumbles in Eastern Europe.
1991	The Soviet Union breaks into separate states.
2001	Terrorists attack the World Trade Center in New York City and the Pentagon in Washington, D.C.
2004	A tsunami in the Indian Ocean destroys coastlines in Africa, India, and Southeast Asia.
2008	The United States elects its first African American president.

Fast Facts

Official name: People's Republic of China

Capital: Beijing

Official language: Putonghua (Beijing dialect of Mandarin)

Beijing

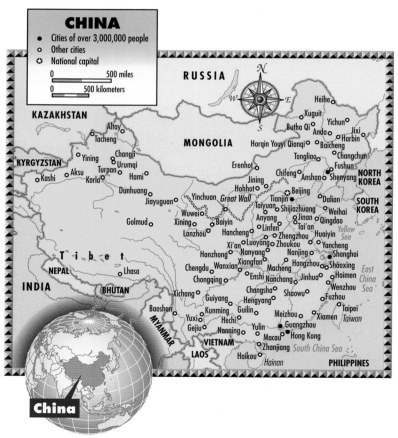

Chinese flag

Official religion:	None
National anthem:	"March of the Volunteers"
Government:	Single-party Communist government
Chief of state:	President
Head of government:	General Secretary of the Communist Party
Area:	3,750,000 square miles (9,700,000 sq km)
Latitude and longitude of geographic center:	03.23°E, 35.33°N
Bordering countries:	Russia and Mongolia to the north; Vietnam, Laos, Myanmar (Burma), India, Bhutan, and Nepal to the south; North Korea to the east; Pakistan, Afghanistan, Tajikistan, Kyrgyzstan, and Kazakhstan to the west
Highest elevation:	Mount Everest, 29,035 feet (8,850 m) above sea level
Lowest elevation:	Turpan Depression, 505 feet (154 m) below sea level
Highest average temperature:	Turpan, with average July highs of around 116°F (47°C)
Lowest average temperature:	Harbin, with average January lows of around −1.1°F (−18.4°C)

Yangtze River

Giant panda

Currency

National population:	More than 1.3 billion	
Population of largest cities:	Shanghai	18 million
	Beijing	13.2 million
	Guangzhou	12 million
	Shenzhen	8.6 million
	Tianjin	8.2 million
	Chongqing	7.5 million

Famous landmarks:
- ▶ *Giant Panda Sanctuaries,* Qionglai and Jiajin Mountains
- ▶ *Great Wall,* northern China
- ▶ *Forbidden City,* Beijing
- ▶ *Temple of Heaven,* Beijing
- ▶ *Terra-cotta Army,* Xi'an

Economy: China is a world leader in textiles, electronics, iron, steel, tin, nickel, coal, natural gas, oil, rice, wheat, potatoes, chicken, pork, and fish. It is also one of the world's leading tourist destinations. China's economy is the fastest-growing in the world and second in size only to that of the United States.

Currency: Chinese currency is called renminbi ("people's money"). The basic unit it called the yuan. In 2011, 6.5 yuan equaled 1 U.S. dollar.

System of weights and measures: China uses the metric system for international trade and a Chinese system within the nation.

Literacy rate: 94%

Schoolchildren

Gong Li

Common Chinese words and phrases:		
	Ni hao	Hello
	Zaijian	Good-bye
	Xiexie	Thank you
	Qing	Please
	Zaoan	Good morning
	Wanshang hao	Good evening
	Wanan	Good night

Prominent Chinese:		
	Confucius *Philosopher*	(551 BCE–479 BCE)
	Deng Xiaoping *Communist leader*	(1904–1997)
	Gong Li *Actress*	(1965–)
	Mao Zedong *Political and military leader*	(1893–1976)
	Wang Wei *Poet and painter*	(699–761)
	Yao Ming *Basketball player*	(1980–)
	Zhang Yimou *Filmmaker*	(1951–)

To Find Out More

Books

- Berlatsky, Noah. *China*. Farmington Hills, MI: Greenhaven Press, 2010.

- Heuston, Kimberley. *Mao*. New York: Franklin Watts, 2010.

- Roberts, Jeremy. *Chinese Mythology A to Z*. New York: Chelsea House, 2010.

- Wang, Qicheng. *The Big Book of China: A Guided Tour Through 5,000 Years of History and Culture*. San Francisco, CA: Long River Press, 2010.

- Whiteford, Gary T., and Christopher L. Salter. *China*. New York: Chelsea House, 2010.

- Ye, Ting-xing. *The Chinese Thought of It: Amazing Inventions and Innovations*. Toronto, ON: Annick Press, 2009.

DVDs

- *China: A Century of Revolution*. Zeitgeist Films, 2007.

- *China from the Inside*. PBS Video, 2007.

- *China Rises: A Documentary in Four Parts*. Discovery Channel Home Video, 2008.

- *China's First Emperor*. A&E Home Video, 2008.

- *Wild China*. BBC Video, 2008.

Web Sites

▶ **History for Kids China Page**
www.historyforkids.org/learn/china
*Plenty of great information about
China's long history, plus lots on
people, art, science, philosophy,
economy, and more.*

▶ **National Geographic's China
Site for Kids**
http://kids.nationalgeographic.
com/kids/places/find/china
*Lots of basic information and great
photos.*

Embassies

▶ **Embassy of the People's
Republic of China**
2201 Wisconsin Avenue NW
Washington, DC 20007
303/338-6688
http://www.china-embassy.org/eng/

▶ **Embassy of the People's
Republic of China in Canada**
515 St. Patrick Street
Ottawa, ON K1N 5H3
Canada
613/789-3434
http://ca.china-embassy.org/eng/

Index

Page numbers in *italics* indicate illustrations.

insect life, 34, 38
Internet, 105, 126
irrigation, 40
Islamic religion, 45, 97, *97*

J

jade, 106, *106*
Japan, 51
Jinsha River, *16*
Judaism, 45
judicial branch of government, 57, 63, 64–65, *65*

K

kites, 126, *126*
Kublai Khan, 47, 59

L

languages, 40, 42, 83, 84, 86–89, *86, 87, 88,* 111, 116
Laozi (philosopher), 41, 93, *93*
legislative branch of government, 57, 62, *62,* 63–64, *63*
Li Po, 45
Li River, *14*
literature, 42, 45, 103–105, *105,* 133
livestock, 40, 79
loan words, 89
local governments, 58, 127
Loess Plateau, 19
Long March, 51
Lu Ban, 126

M

Macau, 23, 58, *58,* 84, 88
Manchu Empire, 48
Manchuria, 20

Mandarin Chinese language, 86, 111
mandarin oranges, 31–32, *31*
manufacturing, 21, 52, 71, *72, 73,* 76–77, *76,* 79
Mao Zedong, 50, *50,* 51, 52, *52,* 54, *54,* 67, 71, *71,* 85, 133
maps. *See also* historical maps.
    Beijing, 59
    ethnic groups, *84*
    geopolitical, *11*
    population density, *82*
    resources, *77*
    topographical, *17*
"March of the Volunteers" (national anthem), 66
marine life, *14,* 32, 85
markets, *70, 75, 78*
martial arts, 123
Marx, Karl, 52
metric system, 72
military, 40, 46, 47, *49,* 50–51, 66, 123
Ming dynasty, 47–48
mining, 20, 77, *77,* 79
Mongolian Border Uplands, 19
Mongols, 47, *47,* 48, 59, 84, 85
monsoons, 27, 59
Mount Everest, 17, 18
mulberry trees, 38
museums, 59, 107
music, 66, 104, 109–111, *100, 109, 110, 111,* 116
mythology, 100–101, *101*

N

Nanai people, 85, *85*
Nanjing, 52, 81, 90
national anthem, 66

National Art Museum, 107, *107*
national flag, 53, *53,* 61, *61*
national holidays, 117
Nationalist Party, 49–50, 51, 52
National People's Congress (NPC), 62, *62,* 63–64, *63*
Nie Er, 66
Ningxia Hui region, 58
Niujie Mosque, *97*
Nixon, Richard M., 66, 67

O

oil industry, 9, 74, 77, 79
Olympic Games, 55, *55,* 122, 123
one-child policy, 81–82, 83, *83,* 84
opera, *100,* 110, *110*

P

Pagoda of Tianning Temple, 59, *59*
Pearl River, 23, *112*
peasants, 51
peonies, 30, *30*
people
    adoption, 83
    birth rate, 81–82
    children, *12,* 75, 81–82, 83, *83,* 84, 85, 86, *109,* 117, *117, 118,* 119, *122,* 124, 125–126
    clothing, 30, 85, 110, *110, 117,* 124, *124,* 125, *125*
    drinking water, 27, *27*
    education, 11, *12,* 35, 42, 81, 82, 89, 116–117, *117,* 125
    elderly, 82, *118,* 119
    "elite society," 53
    employment, 9, 11, 75–76, *76,* 77, *112,* 117, 127, *127*

Meet the Author

WIL MARA IS THE AUTHOR OF MORE THAN 120 BOOKS, both fiction and nonfiction, for readers of all ages. He began his writing career in the 1980s with a manuscript for TFH Publications—at the time, the world's leading producer of animal-related books—and joined their editorial staff shortly thereafter. Five years and twenty-two TFH titles later, he moved into the editorial department at Harcourt Brace while starting in fiction with several ghostwritten titles for Albert

Whitman's popular Boxcar Children mystery series. *Wave*, his inaugural novel for adults, was published in 2005. It sold out its first printing in less than sixty days and earned him a New Jersey Notable Book Award. He now writes a series of disaster thrillers for Macmillan Publishing, as well as a line of suspense novels. Mara also manages to see his wife and children in the hallways and stairwells of his New Jersey home from time to time.

Photo Credits